THE PERFECT MALE VOICE CHOIR

....well, nearly perfect

Paull Robathan

Taunton Deane Male Voice Choir

Title with express permission of composer Denys Hood

Cover design by: David Stewart Kelly

Errata

Pages 52, 67

Please read Rotterdam,
not Amsterdam

This history of Taunton Deane Male Voice Choir is dedicated to all the choir members through the 75 years of our existence, to the musical directors and accompanists, and to the supporters who have all made this journey possible, and so enjoyable.

We would like to record our thanks for the support of our patrons and sponsors who have been such great enthusiasts and partners over the decades.

David Gill, our President, took over the mantle from his father Willie Gill. Between them they have presided over the choir for 51 years. Our 75th Anniversary is also David Gill's 40th year – an amazing achievement and one that has given the choir a strong backbone.

The contents of this book have been drawn together from many sources.

A major contribution has been from "Sixty Years of Singing" a history of the choir's first 60 years put together by Jack Dennis, aided and abetted by Dr Francis Burroughes.

The last 15 years history, and additional material throughout the 75 years, has been gleaned from many personal reflections, material from Voice-Male (the choir's newsletter) and from press reports of events that the choir has taken part in.

CONTENTS

.

FOREWORD

David Gill, President

My family involvement with the choir started in 1969 when my father Councillor Willie (Bill) Gill was Mayor of Taunton. The late Founder Secretary, Cyril Salway, made a beautiful oak plaque for him with coloured paintwork commemorating his Year of Office and incorporating the Defendamus* Coat of Arms. My father regularly attended choir rehearsals and sang with 'the boys'.

> *Defendamus - we shall defend - refers to the siege of Taunton in 1644/5 when Taunton refused to surrender to the Royalists. It was also the name of a pageant in 1928 and is still incorporated in the Abbeyfield Taunton Defendamus Society, retirement and assisted living; the choir over the early years regularly raised funds for this worthy cause. An anthem with the same name was composed in 1928 by Laurence Tanner with words by Major MF Cely Trevelyan. The choir and audience sang this anthem at Rowbarton in 1950.

Following his sudden death in 1980 the choir kindly organised a special Tribute Concert at St. Andrew's Church - all proceeds were put towards a Memorial Gift for Holy Trinity Church where he had sung for 50 years.

Early in 1981 I was elected President of your wonderful Choir and have since tried to regularly attend our Committee Meetings, Chair our AGM's and host VIPs at our principal Concerts.

The Choir can be very proud of the vast sums of money they have raised over many years (all for good causes) and of the terrific pleasure they have given to countless audiences. I am so grateful for support given to me by the Choir during my Year of Office as Mayor of Taunton Deane in 1978 / 79.

It has been my good fortune to work closely with some really special Choir Members (Chairmen and Secretaries in particular) who have all given unstinting service and who have helped in making the Choir what it is today.

Over a number of years Choir Dinners and other social functions have been organised (some with interesting speakers and entertainers); wives, partners and friends have joined us on these occasions and much fellowship has been shared.

Since the Covid lockdown nearly all Clubs have gone through a very difficult period and indeed many have closed down altogether. We are greatly indebted to past Chairman Paull Robathan and Secretary Richard Salter for their amazing efforts to 'keep the show on the road'.

Very few organisations can boast that they have celebrated Silver, Ruby, Golden, Diamond and now 75th Anniversaries and we should all be extremely proud of their achievement and try to give all the support possible to ensure the Choir's successful future.

My warmest congratulations, thanks and best wishes to everyone connected in any way with our Choir - keep up the good work.

David Gill
October 2021, President since 1981

1 INTRODUCTION

Taunton Deane Male Voice Choir was formed in 1946. Originally called Wessex Male Singers, the choir shared its birth with the resurgence of choirs such as Treorchy and others that marked the new post-war era with optimism and a return to singing. Since 1946 the choir has grown in numbers and in quality of performance maintaining a generous and welcoming face for new members.

Choral singing has many guises, from the sea shanties of the 19th century through to Gregorian chant, from which genres some of our number graduated. All over the world group singing is a chosen pursuit of the young, the old, the capable and the amateur. Singing undoubtedly can improve health, wellbeing and happiness not just for the singer, but also for the audience.

Taunton Deane Male Voice Choir has developed over the last 75 years into a robust and committed group of over 70 singers who dedicate a significant part of their lives to raising funds for charity and creating an environment in which men can feel part of a wonderfully warm and inclusive group of individuals from diverse backgrounds and with a wide range of abilities.

During its seventy five years the Choir has had three names. It started life as the "Wessex Male Singers", perhaps a name chosen to avoid conflict with any of the numerous musical societies in the town whose name began with "Taunton". However, by 1960, Taunton Madrigal Society and Taunton Glee Choir, amongst others, had disappeared, and the name was changed to Taunton Male Voice Choir.

In 1974 Local Government reorganisation stole from Somerset the town of Weston-super-Mare and banished it into exile in the made-up area of Avon. Taunton Rural District Council became the Taunton Deane Borough Council.

Unusually, the Male Voice Choir was ahead of its time, and decided at its 1973 A.G.M. that from the next season the Choir would be known as the now familiar Taunton Deane Male Voice Choir. Therefore it pre-dated the new Borough Council by some nine months. However, it still made use of the old Taunton coat of arms, whose design was first recorded in 1685 (although only officially issued from the College of Heralds in 1934) just before the town was promoted to being the County Town.

The title of this book "The Perfect Male Voice Choir" is not a tribute to our choir's perfection, but to the perfect form that our choir and others have strived for to bring joy and warmth to all involved. Denys Hood, who wrote the song *The Perfect Male Voice Choir* especially for Taunton Deane Male Voice choir included the line "well, nearly perfect" as a balance and we hope that when you have finished reading this history you will be as proud as we are of how the choir has served the community of Taunton and the wider area, and intends to continue to do so for many years to come.

Denys Hood has generously confirmed he is happy with our use of the song title for this book. He tells us that he well remembers the first performance by our choir for whom it was commissioned. Mr Hood says the song has generated 'thousands and thousands of copies' and is still going strong. These days (2021) Mr Hood sings with the Bournemouth Symphony Chorus, and we hope to renew our acquaintance with him during our Anniversary celebrations.

1946 was the year that the world was emerging from devastating world war and began looking forward to a brighter future. 2021 shares very similar attributes, the Corona Virus Pandemic has shattered the world's natural order, and only now are we beginning to see the light at the end of the tunnel thanks to vaccination.

We hope that everyone will share in a resurgent and positive period worldwide. The choir will begin concert performance in late 2021 and we are open for new members to join us and for new audiences to share in the joy of Male Voice singing. Our choristers come from a wide area, centred on Taunton, stretching 10 or 15 miles in every direction.

The material for this retrospective on our choir is drawn from a wide range of sources. As editor I have been aided by a wealth of written material, images and personal recollections, much of which has been woven in to what I hope you will feel is a coherent whole. The images are all available on our website www.tauntondeanemvc.com which we recommend you access in parallel with reading this book.

The Choir archive at The Somerset Heritage Centre will be the source of physical artefacts and historical matter, and generally available for public access.

In choosing how to construct this history I have segmented the material into roughly 15 year periods, mainly because our last major celebration was the 60th Anniversary, but also because 75 years splits nicely into 5 chunks of 15 years that I hope you will agree conform to significantly different eras for the world at large and for the choir.

As well as these historical periods the book establishes the background in which the choir operates, Taunton, its history and linkages, and also there are dedicated chapters about our musicians and management who have made the choir what it is today. In some cases information is presented in a different 15 year chapter from the period that might appear appropriate, but I hope that this enhances the readability of the material rather than confuses.

The Choir hope that you enjoy reading our history, and that some of you may want to join us in our journey either as singers or supporters. Either way contact the choir through our website or come to one of our rehearsals at The Temple Methodist Church in Taunton on a Wednesday evening.

There are hundreds of photographs of the choir in various periods of its existence, and a number of newspaper articles related to the events described in this book. Certainly there are too many to include them all, and difficult not to include them all, so apologies if your favourite memory is not included here; it is in the archive or on the website.

The collection of print-only and electronic Voice-Male spans a period of nearly 25 years and is rich with choir information and articles about concerts and other memorable events in the choir's life. Voice-Male also allows for members to present their own views and historical recollections. Malcolm Phillips, who sadly passed away in this Anniversary year, wrote in Voice-Male April 2007 about choirs and their musical debt to Wales. The opening lines suffice to characterise the piece, which is recommended reading:

"Is it true that all Welshmen can sing? NO, of course it isn't. There are at least 1.5 - 2% who can't hit a note for a Penclawdd cockle, but these chaps are often able to live moderately fulfilled lives doing committee work. (editors note - the Penclawdd cockle from the Swansea Bay area is one of Wales' most popular snacks)

"That most famous scribe and scholar Giraldus Cambrensis (Gerald of Wales) noted in the 12th Century that the Welsh liked nothing better than singing" (apart from a couple of other activities) and he noted that Welsh choirs sang in parts with resultant mellifluous harmonies."

It is this harmonious and uplifting part-singing that the Male Voice Choirs of the world aspire to, and Taunton Deane Male Voice Choir strive along with them.

This history finishes with the Formal Dinner on October 16th 2021 that celebrated the 75th Anniversary, and also the imminent return to singing in public. Please follow us to see how the return to some form of normality is going!

2 THE LONG DAY CLOSES

Each of the chapters of our history derives its title from a song the choir has performed. In this case *The Long Day Closes* was set to music by Arthur Sullivan (of Gilbert and Sullivan) in 1868. The lyrics by Henry Fothergill Chorley are a part song for several voices and represent the mourning of death. The choir first sang this song in 1992, the year the film of the same name was released. The film depicted a shy boy whose life was enhanced by snippets of music and film dialogue and as Stephen Holden of the New York Times wrote in 1993 in his article 'Turning a Gloomy World into a Sunny One' "evoke a postwar England starved for beauty, fantasy and a place to escape". A fitting backdrop to the beginning of the immediate post-war era.

My trawl through the choir's newsletter Voice-Male tells me that the much talked about trip to Jersey in 2001 saw Trinity sing *The Long Day Closes* – much more later (that is printable these days) about the Jersey Trip!!

1946 was a wet year as recorded by the Meteorological Office, London. A fine spring was followed by outstandingly high rainfall in June, August, September and November. There were frequent severe gales especially in the South West in late September.

The winter of 1946 / 47 was severe in economic and living conditions with major disruption to businesses, widespread starvation of animals, and large snow drifts in early 1947 still haunting the memory of many to this day.

Amidst all this gloom October 1946 was noted for a spell of generally dry but colder weather. It was into this dry cold spell that there emerged the choir that is now called Taunton Deane Male Voice Choir.

On October 2nd 1946 a meeting was held at the 6, North Street office of the District Labour Party in Taunton. The minutes of that meeting, contained in our archive, record that the purpose was *'forming a Male Choir to replace that of the Taunton Trades Council now disbanded'*. At the meeting there were eight attendees

Councillor F E Norris,	P J Hingston,
R W Bowditch,	J Harris,
P W Webber,	H O Cook,
W Corrick	C W Salway.

Councillor Norris was elected Chair and recounted the history of the Trades Council Choir which although it had failed to *"take on"* had convinced him that there was enough enthusiasm in the town to float and maintain a really good choir.

The Trades Council Choir has been formed in 1945 by the same Fred E Norris. As a member of the Typographical Union his efforts were recognized nationally in The Typographical Circular by Mr H Wilson. I am indebted to Helen Ford, Archive Manager of the Modern Records Centre at University of Warwick for a copy of the journal containing Fred Norris' response to the national reference. It was felt that the labour movement would benefit from a means of creating fast friendships and bringing joy to many, which remain our aims to this day.

During this same immediate post war period another choir was being revived by the owner of Avimo, Mr Herbert Stevens of Bradford on Tone. In a previous employment Mr Stevens had been noted for his musical ability as a fine pianist and once had his own orchestra and 60 strong choir at Sunbeam Motor Car Company. The Avimo choir is remembered as being formed from a core of Welsh employees, but after a short period it was only 10 -12 men strong and had a repertoire that was limited. The choir was disbanded before the Wessex Male Singers was formed.

The new choir to be formed that day in October 1946 came from strong and committed parentage......the General Meeting discussed for some time the possible formation of a choir. Mr Harris moved that the choir should be formed and named "The Wessex Male Singers"; seconded by Mr Bowditch the meeting voted unanimously to establish the new choir.

Chairman:
P. G. BAKER,
Tel.: Taunton 2509

Hon. Conductor:
C. C. OXLAND,
Tel.: North Curry 222

Hon. Treasurer:
K. A. COLES,
12, Fairwater Cottages,
Taunton.

pro bono publico

Hon. Secretary:
C. W. SALWAY,
122, Priory Avenue,
Taunton.

President: VICTOR J. COLLINS, Esq., O.B.E., M.P.

The President of the choir was chosen to be Victor Collins, OBE MP. Mr Collins was the Labour MP for Taunton, having been elected in 1945. He lost his seat in 1950 and remains the only Labour MP Taunton has elected to date. In 1958 Mr Collins was made a Life Peer and served in Harold Wilson's first government.

Officers of the choir were chosen at the meeting, including Honorary Conductor Mr J. Tottle and Accompanist Mrs Morrison. Chapter 8, 'What would we do without our Musicians' celebrates the wonderful musicians that have worked hard to make our choir what it is today.

The Secretary of the choir was Mr Cyril Salway who remained a member of the choir for 60 years until his death in 1996. Cyril Salways' daughters and grandson have very fond memories of the choir. Avril Phillips and her sister Carol Tottle recall enjoying many concerts, socials and outings from the earliest days of the choir's formation. Carol Tottle married Christopher the son of Jeffery Tottle the first conductor. This direct link back to the choir's birth will be celebrated during our anniversary concert in December 2021.

The County Town of Taunton in the year 1946 was immeasurably different from the town of Taunton in 2021. Many of the physical aspects of the town are the same and, particularly in the town centre, the street patterns and buildings are recognisable from post-war photographs, but in seventy five years, a vast new motorway and road system, together with huge housing and commercial developments, have swelled the size of Taunton town from a population of about 30,000 to over 70,000. The wider Taunton Deane how has a population of 115,000 and rising.

In 1946 the Radio and the Cinema (here were three in the town) were the means of popular entertainment. Television could hardly be said to be even in its infancy, and for many people the only local musical activity centred around the annual productions of the Operatic Society and the two concerts of the Choral Society.

Popular musical culture was represented by local dance bands in the County Hotel Ballroom, or sing-alongs in the pub, accompanied by a doubtful piano. Gramophone records were still brittle, played for a few minutes only, and likely to shatter if they were dropped. You could listen to the Home Service or, a little later, the Light Programme on the Wireless.

As late as 1951, according to the Census returns, 23% of houses in Taunton were still without flush toilets. Many of the basic necessities of life, including petrol, were still strictly rationed. In any case, only a small minority of the population owned cars. The bicycle, or public transport, were the common means of travel, and in those happy pre-Beeching days, it was possible to journey to virtually every other sizeable town and village in Somerset by real trains which emitted steam and smoke.

Taunton station was designed by Isambard Kingdon Brunel and opened in 1842. Many local people were employed by the Great Western Railway. In 1932 a two storey goods warehouse was opened. In 1946 a marshalling yard was opened to the west of Taunton station.

Throughout the period up to 1946 the passenger and freight traffic on the railway grew with branch lines to Yeovil, Chard, Barnstaple and the West Somerset Railway. which is in operation today carrying over 200,000 passengers in a normal year, despite there being no direct rail link to Taunton since 1971 when the Beeching axe finally fell.

Ex-servicemen were returning to civilian life, although National Service would still be claiming young school-leavers for another dozen or so years, but in 1946 there was a feeling of optimism that perhaps, with a new government, life would be better for the general majority of people.

The outbreak of war in 1939 left its mark on every parish in the County and the next 5 years plus were to bring black-out, bombing raids, airfields, evacuees, American troops, nights on Home Guard duty and days in the Land Army, sons and daughters away in the Services with tales of heroism and hardship which affected everyone.

Somerset played a significant part in the war effort and later in our history the choir formed strong links with 40 Commando who took over Norton Manor Camp and are there today. We will hear more of 40 Commando.

In the early part of the war when invasion seemed likely, the Commander-in-Chief Home Forces devised a plan that involved the construction of defence lines to protect the country and in particular London. In Somerset the Taunton Stop Line, from the estuary of the river Parrett to the English Channel at Seaton on the mouth of the river Axe, a continuous lines of forts, mostly sited on the banks of rivers and canals. A number are still visible today.

During the war there were in all 9 battalions of Somerset Light Infantry (SLI). The two regular battalions were in India and Gibraltar, the rest were in the UK, for the most part employed in the early years on coastal defence duties. Latterly all the battalions took part in operations in India, Italy, Greece and North West Europe.

There have been many members of the choir who have served in one of the armed forces over the years. Members have attended military events that have happened around the county as private individuals. However, there is little doubt that the greatest direct contribution that the choir has made to the services has been through the many fundraising concerts that it has given on behalf of service charities such as the Royal British Legion, SSAFA, King George's Fund for Sailors (now the RN/RM charity), the Army Benevolent Fund and RAF Benevolent Fund. A recent example of this was the magnificent Armistice Concert at St. Mary Magdalene Church, Taunton on 27 October 2018 to commemorate the centenary of the end of the First World War, at which the Taunton Deane Male Voice Choir together with Taunton Military Wives Choir and the Royal Air Force Association Band raised many thousands of pounds for the SSAFA charity. Ties between the military and the choir have been strong over the years and remain so.

The minutes of the choir committee often remind us of the wider local scene and by reading between the lines details emerge of daily life of the period. Even the rehearsal venue of the early days of the Choir, the "Rowbarton Adult School" carries a distinct flavour of a previous age. The Adult School evolved out of charitable trusts set up in the late nineteenth century, and by the 1940s came to occupy a wooden building on the corner of Greenway Crescent. Despite its rather formal name, it acted as a local community hall for the area, and housed local societies and interest groups, as well as lectures and classes under the auspices of the Workers Educational Association.

The classes and activities formerly held under the auspices of the Adult School were largely subsumed into evening classes at Somerset College of Arts and Technology (SCAT), and other local educational establishments. Later on in 1956 the Choir affiliated to SCAT, or Taunton Technical College as it then was, in an effort to boost recruitment. The Choir Register for that year is an official evening class register, with the Conductor F. Goodliffe recorded as the Instructor; unfortunately this produced no great influx of new young members and, eventually, in 1994, the Choir decided to withdraw from the association.

3 WE'LL GATHER LILACS

In the early days the Wessex Male Singers were perhaps few in number but made up for it by their dedication and commitment to the choir's cause.

Without hard evidence in the form of recordings it is very hard to guess just what the choir must have sounded like 75 years ago. As far as we know no recordings of the choir have survived before the Golden Jubilee Concert in 1996 (If any reader knows of any please contact the Choir). It has become the custom to record the Choir at every Annual Concert since then and on one or two other occasions also. We can therefore judge the performance of the choir dispassionately on these occasions, but the only evidence we have of performance standards before 1996 are reports of the concerts which are often partisan to say the least.

The Publicity Officer, throughout the Choir's history, often complained that it was difficult to get reports of the Choir's activities into the County Gazette, and often the only way for a concert review to appear was for the Choir to submit one itself. Hence, we should read these reports with a grain or two of scepticism since the aim of the reports was to gain good publicity for the choir. Rather more unbiased criticism can be gleaned from the adjudications of the various Festivals and Competitions that the Choir entered over the years.

Again, these are not likely to be completely unvarnished in their opinions, but by reading them one may get a better impression of the quality of the Choir at a particular point.

As in life, very often, the Choir's shrewdest critics are the Choir wives who regularly support their husbands and attend each concert and who may therefore be the best judges of progress. (In recent years, a number of concert reviews written by wives and supporters have appeared in Voice-Male, the Choir's newsletter.). This is a representative recent sample.....

Concert Reviews by Perceptive Wives

NEVER PERFORM WITH CHILDREN OR ANIMALS

Cathy Crosby reviewed a concert at Combe St. Nicholas.

"'Never perform with children or animals' is every actor's mantra. Disaster or humiliation is inevitable. Happily, the Combe St. Nicholas concert was a delightful exception to the rule.

On the 24th of February, the Taunton Deane Male Voice Choir gave a joint concert with the children of Combe St. Nicholas Primary School and the Kids section of the Chard Light Operatic Society, otherwise known as CLOKS.

"The gentlemen set the evening off to a good start with their rendition of *When the Saints go Marching In* followed by the Gilbert and Sullivan chorus *With Catlike Tread*, finishing with two pieces from Les Miserables in which contrast and diction were good.

"The children, very ably led by Maria Farey, then sang three songs from well known musicals. The singing was slick and some very young children confidently sang the lower parts against the melody.
As well as performing separately, the Farey family performed two pieces with words written by Jemima and Otterley set to music by their father.

"To conclude the first half of the concert, all choirs combined to perform a very different version of *This Old Man*, conducted by Val Hill who, by the end, had four choirs singing in canon—great stuff!

"The gentlemen restarted the concert with *The Green Hills of Somerset* and *Last of the Summer Wine* followed by a couple of plantation songs.

"The older children, who belong to CLOKS , performed some more songs from the shows, and the evening then concluded with a performance of *The (not quite) Perfect Male Voice Choir,* redeemed by what Male Voice Choirs are really good at - hymns! *Gwahoddiad* and *Morte Christe* were tremendous.

To Cornwall – Avoiding Weak Bridge

Pauline Blackmore reports over troubled water

"What a wonderful combination – choirs and Cornwall in bright sunshine (well most of the time!) I don't know who enjoyed Taunton Deane MVC's special weekend more – the men, or the faithful "WAGs". As one of the latter, can I offer a short but big thank you for all that made it so memorable: principally to Tony (Slavin) of course for his awesome feat of organisation; and to everyone on the trip, for such a time of warmth and companionship.

"We will all have our favourite memories! Here are my top three:

"Saturday, Liskeard Methodist Church. The Czech Boys' Choir, especially their colourful and energetic *Trepa No Coqueiro.*

"Sunday, St John's Church, St Austell. A re-vitalised Taunton Deane Male Voice delivering the goods with a revamped programme - up where they belong on a par with their fellow performers, Cornish or Welsh.

"Monday, the Eden Project. Songbirds high in the Mediterranean Biome competing with the choirs; and a real magic moment when the Tideswell men's *African Chant* seemed to bring from thin air a spontaneous distant echo (from some of the George South African Male Choir elsewhere in the dome).

"One mystery though.....there was a choir who performed at Liskeard on Saturday - probably very good, but weren't having a good night. *Ain't nevver bin zeen zince – muss've bin magicked away by they Cornish Piskies!"*

The heading of Pauline Blackmore's piece talks about a weak bridge. Trevor Davies recalled such an event....

"As regards deserting the ladies, it was a dark and stormy night......

"We were scheduled to sing a joint concert at a remote church in a small village in the heart of Bodmin Moor. We set off in our coach, one of Berry's double decker Superfast coaches. The driver may have got lost as it seemed to take ages and we were travelling down ever narrowing lanes seemingly in the heart of nowhere.

"Eventually we reached a hump-backed bridge that we couldn't cross because of our coach's long wheelbase. So as not to block the road the driver managed to reverse in to the mouth of a long disused quarry just back from the bridge. The stone cliffs towered over the bus and everywhere was covered in vegetation.

"After a lot of phone calls, that proved difficult because of the poor signal out on the moor, a relief bus was sent by the organisors. This turned out to be a small rather scruffy 'works' type bus that carried far fewer passengers than our own. By now time was getting on, and there was a danger we would be late for the rehearsal. So only the choristers (plus Hazel) got on the relief bus leaving everyone else behind on the Berry's coach with the promise that the relief bus would go back for them later.

"By this time it was dark, owls were hooting, and there was rustling in the bushes....in the end we did get to the rehearsal just in time, the ladies arrived in time for the concert and we all lived happily ever after."

One of the earliest reviews of the Choir we have is of a concert given in Chard Guildhall in 1949 and reviewed in the County Gazette: "At the Corn Exchange, Chard, on Friday, a concert was given by the Wessex Male Singers of

Taunton, under their conductor Mr. C.C. Oxland. The Bristol Concert Orchestra, under their conductor, Frank Cantell, provided just the right balance to the choral works.

"Included in the items by the Choir were *Britons Sing* by Henry Geehl, the air being the *Trumpet Voluntary* (Purcell), followed by *The Old Woman* (Hugh Roberton), *The British Grenadiers*, *In Absence* (Dudley Buck), and the final group *In a Monastery Garden* (Albert W. Ketelby), *Soldiers Chorus* (Faust) arranged by Henry Tolhurst and *Sleep Baby Sleep* (Brahms) arranged by W. Cotton."

The Music Critic was of the opinion that all the pieces had been rendered in a very fine manner and that the choir were most fortunate in their choice of conductor. The choir were very well trained in expression. The supporting artists included Margaret Morrison, a young and promising violinist, who is to be congratulated on her rendering of two movements from the *Sonata in F* by Handel. Appreciation must be expressed to the accompanist, Betty Morrison.

"The audience of over 200 was most attentive and appreciative."

◆ ◆ ◆

Those members in December 1950 are recorded on a programme from Rowbarton. One singer made it to the concert, but was not on the programme - PG Baker was added and recorded for posterity.

The Festival Of Britain

In 1950 the suggestion was made that there should be a large Choral Concert in September 1951 for which the main choirs of the town would combine to celebrate the Festival of Britain. This Festival was designated as "a tonic for the Nation", and was designed to act as a showcase for the best of British design, architecture, and planning.

The Government concentrated most of its efforts on the South Bank in London, converting a bomb site into the main centre for the Exhibition, with such modernistic temporary buildings as the Dome of Discovery (approximately where the 'London Eye' is sited now), and the 'Skylon', a tapering illuminated shape of no purpose whatsoever, kept upright by a systems of guy wires, so that it appeared, as commentators at the time said, "like the British economy, without visible means of support."

The most permanent legacy of the Festival is the Royal Festival Hall, opened with a concert conducted by Sir Malcolm Sargent in May 1951. Other more local festivals were held in Cardiff, Birmingham, Manchester, Bristol, Belfast, Glasgow and Edinburgh, and the Government hoped that local towns and cities would also sponsor their own activities under Herbert Morrison's guidance.

As it happened, most people decided to travel to London and sample the delights of Battersea Fun-fair themselves, rather than organise their own local efforts and over 14 million people, (not all from Taunton!) visited the Fun-fair and the Guinness clock during the summer of 1951. But the Festival's undoubted success was in encouraging a new approach to design in the early fifties, and for the first time modernism became an acceptable and popular design feature in all areas of daily life.

Taunton, like many towns throughout the country, set up a Festival of Britain committee, but, also like many towns throughout the country, eventually produced few activities and celebrations, and instead organised coach and train excursions to the South Bank.

The Male Voice Choir eventually decided to join in the proposed Concert in June 1951, despite their doubts about its viability. It had been suggested, at a meeting of delegates of the various choirs, that if the proposed concert made a loss, the participating choirs should share it equally. Needless to say, the Male Voice Choir delegate, P.G. Baker, strenuously rejected this suggestion!

The Concert was held on September 27th at Bishop Fox's School. The Male Voice Choir, Taunton Madrigal Society, Taunton Operatic Society, the Somerset Amateur String Orchestra, and the West Somerset Singers took part. The Male Voice Choir sang no fewer than nine items. If other performers followed suit it must have been something of a marathon! Two days later the Taunton Festival of Britain Choir, including several members of the Male Voice Choir, gave a performance of *Messiah* in St. Mary's Church, with soloists Isobel Baillie, Irene Byatt, Eric Greene, and Owen Brannigan.

Among Taunton's other efforts was the creation of a new ornamental garden on some derelict land on the corner of Station and Belvedere Roads by the Parks Department, the erection of entrance gates at the Cheddon Road Playing Field, (paid for by Taunton, Massachusets) and a Festival of Britain Service held in St. Mary's Church.

◆ ◆ ◆

Floods

On the 15th and 16th of August 1952 the Lynmouth Flood disaster claimed 34 lives, and the village was largely damaged and destroyed, following torrential storms. 450 people were made homeless, 165 houses were damaged, and 28 bridges were swept away by the force of the swollen river. Ray Butler, current Baritone, recalls that although he and his parents had moved away from Lynmouth by the time of the flood his Aunt and Uncle still lived in Lynmouth. The police asked Ray's mother if she would like to go and identify her sister's body. Ray went with her for moral suport and its "something I will never forget"

The damage was estimated at a cost of between £3 and £5 million, but the final total was far higher. All over the country special appeals were held. Within a fortnight over £300,000 had been subscribed. The Wessex Male Singers held a special concert in aid of the appeal at Temple Methodist Chapel, and raised the sum of twenty guineas.

Eight years later in 1960 Taunton was to suffer a similar, though less destructive fate, when on the 27th October the worst floods ever experienced in Taunton swept through the lower-lying areas of the town following particularly torrential rain. 298 houses and 150 shops were affected, and one intrepid angler caught a three-foot eel in Station Road.

Taunton Expands

In 1954 the Secretary had moved to the newly built Somerset Avenue, and he records rather piquantly, that at the end of a Committee meeting at his home, "the town dwellers stumbled into the darkness and disappeared into the night."

Taunton of course was rather smaller in area fifty years ago, and Galmington and Bishops Hull were still distinct communities, separated by open fields and unlit lanes from the streetlights of Taunton town.

On the 6th of May 1954 Roger Bannister had broken the four-minute mile at Oxford, so the centre of Taunton was theoretically within a few minutes run of the Secretary's house. Dr. Roger Bannister later became Chairman of the Sports Council, and in September 1973 visited Taunton and the surrounding district, where he officially opened Wellington's new £370,000 Sports Centre.

The Decline in Male Choral Singing in the Area

The following two years record the cessation of Wellington Male Voice Choir and Taunton Madrigal Society, the latter a venerable organisation, dating from the late nineteenth century. The Wellington Choir was founded in the early 1920s, and began with four men singing with an accordion player. From this small start a choir was formed which rehearsed at the British Legion Club, and under its conductor T. Young, achieved considerable success at the Mid Somerset Festival and other competitions, in 1930 coming home with the Challenge

Shield and Bowl, which they continued to win for several years. After the war, their conductor retired to Watchet, and the difficulty of replacing him, together with the difficulties in recruiting new and young members and the lack of a permanent accompanist, had finally persuaded members that the time had come to call it a day. Three or four members joined the Wessex Male Singers but the main advantage for Taunton was the purchase of Wellington's library of music, 120 sets of 25 to 30 copies for the bargain price of £3-10-0d. Some of this is still in the Choir Library, although some has been sent to the County Music Library for storage.

The Taunton Madrigal Society was an offshoot of the Parish Church Choir, and for many years allowed no female participation in its performances. As late as 1954 it was advertising "an annual open smoking concert held in December, and a performance to which ladies might be invited on Shrove Tuesday." It was founded in 1885 "for the cultivation of unaccompanied part singing for male voices." Despite its name, the Madrigal Society also performed glees and catches and nineteenth century part-songs. Treble parts were sung by the trebles of the church choir, and it reached its glory days under the direction of Harold Arthur Jeboult, (1871-1925) and his successor Herbert Knott.

There was also a rival organisation to the Madrigal society, Taunton Glee Choir, equally male-orientated, but which performed rather lighter fare. It's secretary for the last twenty years of its life was the redoubtable P.G. Baker. It folded in the early 1950s, when it amalgamated with the Taunton Madrigal Society, although without Mr. Baker.

On the 24th of April 1958 we could read in the local press
'Taunton Ladies Choir and the Wessex Male Voice Singers combined for the first time on Thursday evening in giving a concert at the Corfield Hall'. Mr. T.S. Jones, who was in his third season as conductor of the Ladies Choir, had now taken over similar charge of the Wessex Male Singers, and their united efforts on this occasion, together with the support of soprano and cello soloists, provided a programme of musical appeal in rich variety. (In 2020 it was announced that the Corfield Hall is to be demolished and replaced with an almshouse sympathetic to the nearby Grade 1 listed St Mary Magdalene Church.)

"The Wessex Male Singers, who have Mrs. Betty Morrison as their accompanist, sang with the piano twice in their first group - Beethoven's *Creation Hymn* and the students' song *Upidee* (arr. Woodgate). A Brahms lullaby, *Sleep Baby Sleep* made the ideal contrast. *Upidee* seemed too solemnly sung for a students' parody of Longfellow's *Excelsior*; smiling faces in the singing of the chorus would have made it more realistic.

"Three accompanied part songs forming the Wessex Singers second group were *A Smugglers' Song* (Arnold Williams), *It's Oh to be a Wild Wind* (Elgar) and *The Eriskay Love Lilt* (arr. Robertson). Kipling's hush-hush lines in the *Smugglers' Song* needed more biting emphasis to be heard as part of the story. There was flowing legato expression in the *Love Lilt*."

One is struck by the length of the concert, since the Ladies Choir sang fourteen songs in four groups. Sonia Morrison, Betty's daughter, played three extended cello pieces and an encore and the soprano soloist sang six songs and 'was deservedly encored.'

Recruitment

Although recruitment featured in several committee meetings, as late as 1960 it was recorded that "there was no urgency to recruit members, and no action should be taken" in regard to any practical efforts at recruiting new members. This was despite the fact that the choir had a membership of 23 and an average attendance of only 16. One can only conclude that the choir still regarded itself, in the words of a 1947 minute, as an association for "self amusement, and entertaining our wives and friends, etc."

This attitude to the choir being a primarily social function was reinforced by the remarkable number of family relationships there were within the choir; fathers and sons, uncles and nephews accounted for about 70% of the choir membership at this time, so that it was no wonder that the members felt it to be a rather exclusive social club, which they did not particularly wish to see disturbed by an influx of new faces.

The close linkages between members is reminiscent of the Welsh Male Voice Choir tradition. Local communities in Wales have formed the foundation of the worldwide Male Voice tradition. This can be evidenced directly in our own choir. Rob Morgan joined Taunton Deane Male Voice Choir in the 1990s, but his first choir was Dowlais in the Rhymney Valley.

Rob considers the biggest difference between England and Wales is that Wales has Eisteddfods – "we grew up singing; if you won your school Eisteddfod you were placed in the Town eisteddfod. Win that and you represented your County. Success at County level brought you to the National Eisteddfod which is held in a different location in Wales each year." Rob tells us he never had a solo voice but he must have got enough seconds and third at town level to be a marked boy.....

Just before Rob's 15th birthday Rob recalls the day a man in grey trousers and a blue choir tie knocked on their front door on High Street, Dowlais. and said "Mrs Dix, I've come to take Rob to choir."

Rob continues "My grandmother was so pleased she threw me in to his arms, slamming the door closed so that she could rush in and tell everyone. The man and I sat on the low forecourt wall with legs dangling over the pavement. He introduced himself and then asked me to repeat a few notes then sing a few phrases. "Just as I was told" he said. We were interrupted by the re-emergence of my Nan. "Will it cost anything?" ..."Only half price until he is 18" came the answer, "but if he is keen and sings well I will cover that." And so Rob was press ganged into the Dowlais Male Voice Choir.

Dowlais had over 100 singers on the books in those days, usually 85 on stage. Dowlais practiced twice a week (Some Welsh choirs practice 3 times a week!). Rob qualified for the tour of America in 1985 by having over 85% practice attendance and over 90% concert attendance. Rob met his future wife Mary on this tour, met here again when Mary came to Dowlais in 1990 with the Canton Ohio choir and they were married in 1991.

Rob and Mary moved to Somerset a week after returning to England from the

21

wedding after singing with Dowlais for 20 years. They settled in the Bridgwater area and Rob worked in Northern Sedgemoor. The local choir was Cheddar MV. Rob "Heard them -very correct and accomplished but no hwyl". Other choirs were too distant. Rob says he felt lost and only sung with choral societies and helping out church choirs.

Rob met Tony Slavin in one of Mary's (Mary Morgan, Rob's wife and the choir's favourite soloist) concerts. "He invited me to a TDMVC concert in the town. I joined immediately thereafter." It may have been a help that Tony Slavin was also from Merthyr like Rob and there was a Welsh "Taffia" to welcome him as there is today.

It is instructive to note that the original Wessex singers were sustained through family and close contacts as were the Welsh choirs. In the recent past the decline in Welsh choir numbers has been put down to high unemployment, and a migration of younger people away from the valleys to university. Those that remain have a long standing close bond of comradeship which is very evident in Taunton Deane Male Voice Choir as we will see when other choir members' reminiscences are presented.

There was no policy for choir members retaining their music to do any practice at home until the early 1980s. This was, at least in part, because of a shortage of music but was a factor in limiting the repertoire. It also explains the frequent references which Conductors made to the fact that the choir found difficulty in learning what we would now regard as a minimal repertoire of perhaps only a dozen songs.

Not until 1988 did the Conductor hope that the choir would be able to carry 16 pieces of music in a season. This was increased to 24 for the Golden Jubilee celebrations in 1995/6, and for the Diamond Jubilee up to forty.

However, as late as 1984 the Conductor wondered if the Choir should not return to the idea of a rehearsal group with not so much emphasis on concerts. This followed a year in which the choir had made eleven concert appearances, which would now hardly be regarded as excessive.

The Choir has normally performed its concerts with a guest soloist. In recent years these have often been young musicians just beginning to make a name for themselves. In its early days, Mavis Staples, described as "guest elocutionist" was a popular choice, and performed at many of the Choir's early concerts. The Choir often performed joint concerts with the Taunton Deane Ladies Choir, particularly as they twice shared the same Conductor, and their repertoire was essentially similar. Another link between the two choirs was that Committee Member Cyril Vian's wife, Betty, was for many years Secretary of Taunton Ladies. More recently, concerts have been shared with the Somerset Hills Chorus, the Apple County Chorus, the New Horizon Singers and the Thamesdown Ladies Choir.

The matter of Choir Uniform had exercised the Committee off and on ever since the Choir started in 1946. Various solutions were offered; at one time the Choir appeared to have a formal uniform of dark suit, (the members' own) with a white shirt and wine coloured bow ties, and an informal uniform of dark trousers, blue shirt, and a matching blue tie. Eventually in 1994, the Committee opted for a navy blazer with the Choir badge in navy and gold, a choir tie, in navy with a gold stripe, and white shirts and charcoal grey trousers. It looked smart and dignified and was expected to remain the preferred option for the foreseeable future.

For many Male Voice Choirs the social aspect is one of the most important reasons for membership. Some Choirs have a similar reputation to Brass Bands. The story that at one Brass Band coach outing to a concert, the instruments were left behind in order to have more space in the luggage compartment for crates of beer may be apocryphal, but it has a grain of truth in it. There can be very much an element of a similar mind-set in male voice choirs. Unusually, however, this seems not to be the case with the present Choir.

A few members will go to their local after a rehearsal on a Wednesday evening, but they are in a minority. No doubt a responsible attitude to drink-drive penalties plays a part in this abstemious regime, and also, to be blunt, the average age of Choir members may have a part.

The choir had remarkably few outings and trips in its earlier years. For the first fifty years of the choir's existence we have the pictures of only two outings by coach, both day trips. The furthest afield that the Choir travelled was to Bristol to take part in the Combined Choirs Festival.

Apart from appearances at the Highbridge Music Festival, the Bristol concerts were for many years the only outing which the Choir undertook, and the rehearsal schedule was dominated by the music selected. The concerts had begun during the war, founded by Leslie Woodhouse, and the Choir first participated in 1949. The concerts were originally held in the Colston Hall, which had escaped the Bristol Blitz, but which tragically burned down just before the end of the War in 1945.

The venue was moved to the Victoria Rooms, until the Festival of Britain gave the impetus for the rebuilding of the Colston Hall in 1951 as the largest concert hall in the South West, and the Massed Male Voice Galas moved back there for the 1952 concert. The fine Harrison and Harrison organ was installed in 1954, and immediately use was made of it for accompanying certain items in the programme. The format of the concerts was to be unchanged during all the years that the Choir attended: a selection of eight or ten Male Voice pieces, accompanied by piano or organ, with a couple of audience-participation hymns, and a soloist, either a vocalist, on one occasion at least Cynthia Glover was engaged, or often an organist. Sandy MacPherson was a popular choice.

Six or eight choirs would take part, and one feature of the concert was that each choir would supply the conductor for one of the concert items. No doubt each choir felt it important that their conductor was seen to be the best. One or two of the larger choirs might be asked to sing their own 'party piece' alone, but we are unable to confirm that Taunton ever joined this elite.

The Choirs which usually attended included Newbridge MVC (Bath), The East Street Baptist MVC (Bristol), Keynsham MVC, Shaftesbury Crusade MVC (Bristol), Admiralty MVC (Bath), Parnall MVC (Yate), and Midsomer Norton MVC. None of these choirs exist any longer.

The first record we have of a Choir Social is in August 1952, when Charles

Oxland reported to the Committee that a friend was meeting the cost of Rowbarton Rooms (St. Andrew's Church Hall) for the Social to be held in October 1952. (One can guess, as most of the members must have done, that the 'friend' was Oxland himself. It cost him £25 7s 8d.).

The idea that the Choir was a social association, with only a peripheral musical raison d'etre, was to dog the Choir for many years, and accounts for the apparent unconcern at the sometimes woefully thin concert programme, and the repetition of items in the repertoire year after year.

On occasion the Choir joined with other Male Voice Choirs to perform a Concert locally. As early as 3rd November 1949 the Choir appeared in a Celebrity Concert with Cullompton Male Voice Choir. The soloist was Gwen Catley, but we have no more information on this intriguing event. Whether it was held in Taunton or Cullompton the Minutes fail to tell us, and Cullompton Male Voice Choir has long been disbanded. In recent times it has become a regular event to share the billing with another choir, either Male Voice or often Ladies' and Mixed choirs.

From its earliest days the Choir entered the Taunton Music Festival year each year, despite the fact that particularly after 1954 it was often the only Male Voice Choir competitor. The Choir also travelled to Highbridge, where again it was often the only entrant in a class. More rarely, the Choir entered the Mid Somerset Music Festival, held since 1952 at Bath. Here there was generally more competition, perhaps Swindon or Chippenham Male Choirs attending, or one or two Bristol based Choirs. A more recent visit to the Mid Somerset Festival will be discussed later.

4 BACK TO THE SIXTIES

The Committee sometimes discussed the seating arrangements at Concerts. In 1960 the Committee decided that the Choir would sing in four rows, each part to a row, with first tenors at the front. While the numbers in the choir remained small and fairly evenly balanced, this was fine, except that one or two first tenors were rather taller than some of the first basses, and so seeing the Conductor must have posed a problem for those shorter singers in the third and fourth row, but it is also interesting to note that, in the same year, at the A.G.M., the Choir as a whole agreed that standing to sing produced a better effect. One can only conclude, incredible though it may seem, that the Choir had performed sitting down before this!

Towards the end of the fifties, the choir began to consider their commitment to the Colston Hall Concerts. Here is the Bristol Evening Post's review of the concert held in February 1958:

"Once again, on Saturday, the Colston Hall was less than half full for an enjoyable concert by the Massed Male Voice Choirs of Bristol and District. Among the artists were Cynthia Glover (soprano) and Daphne Spottiswoode (piano) – an additional attraction. A varied programme of considerable local interest then, but which can only draw a fraction of the local inhabitants......

"Ballads predominated, with traditional pieces such as *Upidee* and *The Tarpaulin Jacket.* There was a refreshing buoyancy evident in the lighter side, and yet for me, the most satisfying thing was the deep-throated power and sustained majesty of the opening *Creation's Hymn.* This power might have been more fully exploited with the inclusion of more choral music."

A report on the same concert contributed to the Somerset Gazette was more of a factual statement about the involvement of the Wessex Male Singers with conductor T.S. Jones and accompanist Betty Morrison, but ended in a complimentary fashion:

"The programme concluded with Doris Arnold's arrangement of *The Holy City* which was movingly sung by the massed choirs with organ accompaniment."

The Colston Hall Concerts had made a substantial loss in 1955 and had not broken even since. Taunton withdrew after the 1962 event and the concert was finally abandoned after 1965 when more and more choirs, for various reasons, stopped attending.

In 1963 at the A.G.M. it was proudly stated that "three concerts were arranged, and all had taken place despite the severe weather." The severe weather started on Boxing Day, 1962, and lasted until the 4th March 1963, between which dates most of Britain was under snow. The winter of 1946-1947 had been snowier, with deeper drifts, but 1962-1963 was far colder, in fact the coldest winter in England and Wales since 1740. The blizzard hit the South-West region overnight on 29th.-30th. December, and drifts up to 18 feet deep were recorded in some places. Villages around Taunton were cut off, some for several days. Roads and railways were blocked, telephone wires were brought down and stocks of food ran low. Farmers couldn't reach their livestock, and thousands of sheep, ponies and cattle starved to death, particularly on Dartmoor and Exmoor.

But more cheerfully, in 1963, a new pop sensation performed twice at the Odeon Cinema. The Music Critic of the Somerset County Gazette was at a loss to understand why they should have been invited a second time, when their performance was so "amateurish". "Much to be preferred were our own local musical talents of the Taunton Ladies Choir, the Choral Society, and the Taunton Orchestral Society." One wonders what became of "The Dynamic Beatles", as the group called themselves on their first visit as a supporting act. They visited the town yet again in 1967 when they patronised Smedley's Fish and Chip Shop in Roman Road after meeting Amy and James Smedley on a bus to Newquay Cornwall to film their 'Magical Mystery Tour'. Scenes for the group's Hard Day's Night film in 1964 had been shot at the West Somerset Railway in Crowcombe.

As late as 1971 the Conductor felt that six concerts a year was the limit that the Choir could perform. It was not until the late sixties that recruitment became a more pressing matter, when in 1967 Douglas Shepherd mentioned particularly that tenors were needed, although in the following year he remarked that they did not require an influx of bass members.

In 1962 the choir changed its name to Taunton Male Voice Choir to strengthen ties with the town. In 1974 the name was changed once more, this time to Taunton Deane Male Voice Choir, in an attempt to broaden appeal.

In 1962 the Choir had organised a dinner at Maynard's Café, and it was repeated in 1964, at the lavish cost of 7/6d a head, including table wine. In 1972, as part of the Silver Jubilee celebrations another Choir dinner was held, but on this occasion the result was disappointing, for what reason we are not told.

At the Golden Jubilee in 1996 instead of a Dinner, a Sunday lunch was held at the end of the season, which became an annual fixture in the social calendar for several years, until it was replaced with a more informal barbecue, held at a member's house, Alf Anstee or Dr John Crosby in recent times.

In 1968 the Annual Concert was held jointly with the Wellington Silver Band. The Silver Band can trace its history back, through the Wellington Town Band, to 1887, when it was in turn formed by a group of players from the Wellington Volunteer Band, attached to the 8th. Somerset Volunteer Rifle Corps, founded in the town in 1860.

The Annual Concert was at this time usually held in April, and was repeated a week or so later at Court Fields School, Wellington. It marked the end of the Male Voice Choir season, and the beginning of the Band's season. The sharing of the programme with the Band continued up to 1994. At first these joint concerts were held in Priorswood (St. Augustine's) School in Taunton, but later the concert moved to St. Andrew's Church, and was latterly particularly held in support of Abbeyfields.

The repeat concert in Wellington moved from Court Fields School to the Great Hall of Wellington School in 1984. It became associated with fund-raising for the Wellington Branch of the Royal National Lifeboat Institution, and organised by Philip Threlfall, a Committee
Member and for a year Secretary of the Choir. In the last few years the concert was often relayed by closed circuit television to the Wellington Cottage Hospital next door to the school.

The format of the programme was invariably that each group would perform a selection of items in each half, and then Choir and Band would combine for a final audience- participation hymn. In 1993 and 1994 this was varied slightly by the Choir and Band combining in performances of Gounod's *Soldier's Chorus*, and Wagner's *Pilgrim's Chorus*, with Brass-Band parts arranged by the Choir conductor, The limited nature of suitable items for combined performances was a serious handicap.

5 ANTHEM

1974 was the year the choir changed its name from Taunton Male Voice Choir to Taunton **Deane** Male Voice Choir. It was also the year that the contract was let for the new service station on the M5 at Cutsey, named as Taunton Deane Services.

The M5 is a road frequently travelled by Male Voice Choirs. The excellent Cornish choirs travel the country and often stop at Taunton Deane. The Cornwall Male Voice Choir Festival, held every two years unless circumstances such as Covid-19 intervene, sees a veritable convoy of choirs from the rest of the UK and from further afield.

Our choir is well used to being described as the choir named after a service station, and we take it in good heart. Being known is the key thing, and its a great jumping off point for connecting with other choirs.

Four Lanes Choir from Redruth stopped at the services in 2017 and their website records that eight other choir buses were there at the same time and the end result was 200 voices singing their hearts out. So maybe the Taunton Deane Services is a worthy partner with the choir in preserving the Taunton Deane name.

Chapter 9, Taunton and Taunton Deane, presents the history of the local area and its changing titles and geography over the centuries.

Taunton Deane is immortalised in an old Somerset song *Richard of Taunton Deane*. The sheet music arranged by J.L Molloy is to be found in libraries around the world including the National Library of Australia.

We are fortunate to not only have the sheet music (seen below) but also a video clip of one of our own, Tony Osmond, singing his version of the song *Urchard of Taunton Deane* at St Andrews Church in Rowbarton. Evan Williams, who recorded the video, tells us that it was Tony's party piece and he often performed it during the afterglow, especially in Cornwall.

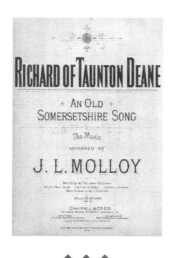

◆ ◆ ◆

The Reg Griffiths Singers

The late Tom Parker, a member of the Choir since 1971, a Committee member, and Treasurer from 1979 to 1982 in the early eighties formed an 'Afternoon Glee Club'. This group of members met for their own pleasure during the week. Eventually they gained enough confidence to sing in public, and by 1986 were performing at about half a dozen occasions during a year.

Tom had persuaded the late Barbara Gimblett to act as accompanist, a post she filled for the next dozen or so years until failing eyesight forced her retirement in 1990. Tom Parker continued to lead the group into his eighties, but his sight deteriorated and Reg Griffiths, who had joined the Afternoon Group when he joined the main choir in 1984, took over the leadership of the group in 1986 identifying the need for a small group of singers to go round to the numerous elderly and disabled groups and societies which meet in and around the town of Taunton. Such clubs are often looking for an hour's entertainment for their members during an afternoon, and Reg organised the concert party to entertain at venues in the town and district. Most of these entertainments happen during the day, which precluded some members of the main choir from taking part, and in any case many venues are very small and cannot hold a large choir of any more than a dozen or fifteen singers.

One or two members, who had retired from singing with the main choir, still felt able to lend their support for an afternoon session once or twice a month. The need this group filled can be judged from the fact that by 1991 it performed at 18 venues during the season, and it often had a busier schedule of engagements than the main choir, with several venues demanding a repeat booking year after year.

The entertainment consisted of numbers from the main choir repertoire, with which the members are familiar, and then one or two individuals also performed a 'party piece', perhaps a song or a monologue to add variety to the programme.

The Afternoon Group gave its services free, but invariably they came away with a donation for their expenses, which all went to the main choir's music funds. Usually this group raised a figure of two or three hundred pounds each year, for which the choir members were all very grateful.

On the death of Reg after a short illness at the start of the 2001 season Alan Richards took over fronting the group. Here he talks about the Reg Griffiths Singers in August 2005:

"The choir is made up of mainly senior, retired, members of the main choir but a few younger members continue to filter through. We sing mostly in the afternoons for almost any organisation that invites us. In fact, it our proud boast that we will sing for anyone that we can lock in a room for about an hour! Our audiences can vary in number from over a hundred down to the proverbial 'one-man-and-his-dog'. It doesn't seem to matter to us, I can always depend on the support of this wonderful band of men who give so freely of their time to entertain so many. We performed in excess of 20 concerts each season in all kinds of venues; village halls, stroke clubs, blind associations, over 60's, residential & nursing homes, churches etc, raising money by donation for our choir music fund or direct to other charities.

"The objective of bringing enjoyment to our audiences, whilst enjoying ourselves, also promotes the main Choir and keeps Male Voice singing alive for many people. The fact that we get invited back each year must be an indication that we are satisfying our aims .

"Just prior to Reg's death the most notable event was the retirement of our accompanist, that wonderful lady Barbara Gimblett. She retired at the age of 90, a remarkable achievement, due to failing eyesight. She had played for the group since its formation and she will never be forgotten. Barbara was expert on piano, organ and even our small keyboard that she hated because her fingers didn't fit the small keys. She will also be remembered for her sense of humour and precise musical timing. Then we were fortunate to recruit our present accompanist, Dora Brooks who is aided by Joan Saunders. They are both providing a sterling service and generously giving of their time. They are greatly appreciated by choir members.

"When Reg passed away we already had a long list of engagements to fulfil. We decided to retain the name in his memory and because that's how people and organisations remembered us, and I volunteered to 'front' the group. Reg was going to be a difficult character to replace, he was larger than life, wonderful with people and gave so much to the group over a long period.

"However life goes on; our prayers were answered when Audrey Silke volunteered to conduct us and we had a new lease of life. Although still singing mainly traditional male voice music, we decided to widen our repertoire and scope as an entertainment group. We now include appealing pieces that Audrey arranges together with our ever-expanding individual talents of solos and duets, poetry and monologue and the occasional joke or two.

"We regularly put between 12 to 18 singers on the stage and over a season nearly half of the main choir have sung in the group at least once. The pleasant problem I have is trying to contain Audrey's enthusiasm. She does so much for us and believes that nothing is beyond our singing abilities. If only that were true!"

The Choir was very fortunate to have the Reg Griffiths Singers, a thriving group of dedicated, good humoured older members who enjoyed each others company and gave so much pleasure to others.

There are many amusing stories of the Afternoon Group's adventures. On one occasion they turned up as arranged one afternoon to sing for a group in Taunton, only to find that the organisers had mistaken the day and there was virtually no audience. The organisers went out into the nearby car park, and eventually recruited an audience of about half a dozen and a dog, who were persuaded to hear the afternoon group sing their concert with an offer of a free cup of tea. It is recorded that the dog was very appreciative!

Liz Bell joined the choir as accompanist in 1981. She said "A friend from Temple Methodist Church asked me if I would be prepared to help out playing for the Taunton Deane Male Voice Choir, conducted by Chris White, as they had no accompanist and urgently needed one. It was a voluntary role which certainly removed some pressure to 'perform perfectly'! I was out of practice having had a break from teaching and was at that time looking after three small children, a live-in Grandpa, and in loco parentis for fifty plus boys in a boarding house at an independent school. The commitment of my playing skills, regular service and support lasted a little longer than envisaged however – nineteen seasons to be precise!

"But neither could I have anticipated just how much I received in return over the years. There was ample opportunity to improve my piano playing, backing up a music making group which gave joy to so many people with its concerts – always fundraising for some worthwhile cause, so one felt one's time was so well spent.

"I remember the tolerance and appreciation of my conductors. There were times when everything was not entirely straightforward. Some pianos which I was required to accompany on, before the choir bought a portable Yamaha Clavinova, were beyond their sell-by date! Sometimes vision was restricted, and on one occasion at the Albemarle Centre the choir was announced with a flourish after which all the lights were switched off except the central spot on the men, leaving me to fumble and improvise a line and a half of introduction totally unable to see any music! I soon learnt to carry with me a soft cushion, a lamp plus extension lead, the usual cough sweets, water bottle and biscuits; also a wonderful wooden backing stand to support my music, specially crafted for me by Wyn Davies, the then Chairman. I was treated royally by "My Men", and enjoyed friendship, fun, and being totally spoilt – for example being driven to concerts and escorted underneath umbrellas if the weather was inclement.

"Memorable moments abound. The Annual Concert was always a special occasion, formerly shared with the Wellington Silver Band in the '80s, firstly at the old St. Augustine's School before it was knocked down, then St. Andrew's church and the Brewhouse. Everyone looked very smart in their uniforms, all on best behaviour and over the years trying to sing without music. We visited many local churches and village halls, and often were supplied with very generous refreshments afterwards which I loved as playing made me hungry. The Choir visited Cardiff Arms Park for massed Male Voice Choir singing – what an experience! And one year we did an audition for the Sainsbury's Choir Of The Year competition. Our conductor, Francis Burroughes, during his years worked very hard to improve the standard of performance and the numbers in the choir."

John Blackmore joined the choir in 1984. He overlapped with some of the very original choir members such as Cyril Salway.

John recalls "I hadn't remotely thought about joining any choir. My only choir experiences were at grammar school and the newly formed Churchstanton church choir when I was still quite young. Neither were particularly positive experiences!

"In 1984 a friend who taught at Heathfield said he had been approached by a colleague to join a Welsh Male Voice choir in Taunton. This colleague turned out to be Wyn Davies who was then the chair of Taunton Male Voice Choir (as they were then known).

"My mate, Gwyn Foster,had been singing in the school's staff choir so Wyn knew he could sing. Gwyn asked me to join too as he was very nervous about it and had heard me sing in church! I said I couldn't join a **Welsh** choir. However after checking that it wasn't in fact a Welsh choir, I couldn't really say No!

"We popped along to a concert at Priorswood School where about 24 choristers sang to a small audience and after that we decided to join. We were both put into the baritones and were mentored by the redoubtable Geoff Ede. That first rehearsal was an eye-opener - they didn't just sing melody they sang in parts!! I concentrated like mad and suddenly it was 9:30pm and all over - two hours had seemed to last about 20 minutes as the time just flew past!

"Gywn eventually moved to the basses and we practised together by his piano to get up to scratch. No practice tapes/CD's/Matrix back then. It was just a few years later when, after we suggested it, I was tasked with achieving it.

"Little did I know then that as one of the youngest in the choir when I joined, I would stay for 37 years outlasting everyone else to become, currently, the longest serving member of the choir!"

John has been a core element of the choir's increasing professionalism and firm foundations through his work on creating practice tapes, as Concert Secretary, editor of Voice-Male and an ever present and supportive front row Baritone.

◆ ◆ ◆

40 Commando and Taunton - A Special Relationship

The association with 40 Commando Royal Marines and Taunton is now so close that it is a surprise to learn that it only started in 1985 when the Commando moved here from Plymouth. There is also a link with the choir since the first Commanding Officer to assume command after that move was Alan Hooper, an established member of the baritone section and the contributor of this piece.

The Royal Marines considered themselves very fortunate to take over the excellent Norton Manor Camp from the Army situated close to the County Town and with access to the Quantocks (ideal for yomping!). The Marines soon adapted to life in the Taunton area, started to buy houses - and to marry local girls. Now, over 35 years later there is a large number of former Royal Marines who have made Taunton their home and Norton Manor Camp is well established as part of the Royal Marines estate in the West Country which includes Plymouth, Barnstaple and Exmouth. However, this was not always the case as for a long time the Camp was included amongst a number of Defence Estates which had been identified for 'disposal.' Following strong resistance from Taunton Deane Borough Council and a persuasive presentation in 2019 from the then Commanding Officer (Lieutenant Colonel Paul Maynard) to the Secretary of State for Defence, Gavin Williamson MP, the Minister, reversed the decision. He was impressed by the excellent relationship with the community, proximity to local training areas, strategic transport links and future potential. It is fair to say that a sense of relief was felt in Taunton, and by the Royal Marines, that common sense had prevailed and people could now get on with strengthening that special relationship.

The relationship did not just happen but was slowly built up over the years. In 2003 this resulted in the Commando being granted the significant honour of the Freedom of Taunton. It gives the Unit 'the right to parade through Taunton with a marching band, Colours flying and bayonets fixed.' This honour sits alongside the 1946 grant of Freedom of the Borough to the Somerset Light Infantry.

The normal pattern of life for the Commando is to spend half of the year away from Taunton. Over the years this has included exercises around the world, including Norway, the Mediterranean, the Middle East and operational tours in Belize, Iraq and Afghanistan. It was the tours in Afghanistan that brought the people of Taunton and the Marines closer together, during the bitter campaign in that country, epitomised by a harrowing tour in 2010 when, very sadly, 14 Royal Marines lost their lives. To stand amongst the crowd in the centre of Taunton when the Commando marched through the town after that operational tour was a proud and emotional experience for both the Royal Marines and the people of Taunton. That was the moment that Taunton welcomed the Commando as 'one of their own'.

During the time that the Commando has been based in Taunton they have undertaken three operational tours in Afghanistan and two in Iraq. However, there is another side to soldiering which is associated with 'peace keeping', and in this 40 Commando has excelled. Each year a unit from each of the Armed Services is awarded the Sword of Peace in recognition of activities that go above and beyond their normal role that improves relations with communities, either within the UK or overseas. In 2019 the Commando was awarded the Firmin Sword of Peace for an unprecedented fourth time - more than any other unit since the award was established in 1966 by Wilkinson Sword. Previous Swords had been won by 40 for humanitarian work whilst on operations in Borneo (1966), Northern Ireland (1972) and Cyprus (1984). This fourth one was for significant contribution to the UK Government's crisis response to the Caribbean hurricane disaster in 2017. And so, on a bright sunny day in April 2019, with the other three swords on parade, 40 Commando was presented with this latest addition by General Sir Gordon Messenger, Vice Chief of the Defence Staff, then the most senior serving Royal Marine and a former Commanding Officer of 40 Commando, who also lives in the Taunton area.

The close association also extends to the choir. In October 2016 one of the Commando officers was at an official function for 'Britain in Bloom' held at the county cricket ground sponsored by the Mayor at which the choir sang a couple of numbers. He was so impressed that he asked whether the choir would be prepared to sing at the Remembrance Parade at Norton Manor Camp. As a result, on a cold dry day the following month some 30 choir members assembled at the Camp and had the rare privilege of witnessing the whole of the Commando on parade. For some members it was the first time that they had been inside Norton Manor Camp, let alone watch a parade of this size - so the challenge was on! Could our choir of middle aged men wearing their choir uniform match the smartness of the Royal Marines in their blues? We sang our hearts out, however, as it was in the open air we did not know whether we had sung well enough. The answer came from the Naval Chaplain taking the service when he challenged the Marines, all 500 of them, to match the sound of our small choir!

That experience was only matched by the unique experience of singing with the Royal Marines Band at Queens College in support of Go Commando in July 2017. It was at the afternoon rehearsal that we realised that we were in the company of experienced professional musicians from arguably the best military band in the world - so no pressure! With impressive flexibility their Director of Music 'adjusted' to our level and the result was a really good combined performance of which the choir was justifiably proud.

All of this goes to show that the association between the Royal Marines and Taunton is a very special one. A large number of Marines have retired in the area and the County Town has welcomed them into the community and adopted 40 Commando as 'its own.' This association has also extended to the choir as there are now four Royal Marines in our ranks: Alan Hooper, Gerry Wells Cole, Richard Walker and Tim Webster. The attraction of joining such a close knit organisation as Taunton Deane Male Voice Choir with such a strong connection to the Royal Marines makes for a special bond which is strengthened even more when we sing with the Military Wives Choirs (from Taunton most often, but also from Yeovilton Naval Air Station).

1988 was the year that the choir reached the pinnacle of its decade of attendance at Highbridge Festival of the Arts.

The Honours Certificate below was awarded for performances of *Standing on the Corner*, where the adjudicator's comments were "Fine Voices - a warm blend - good lilt and tempo", but a comment was made about Copies! The second song, *Jacob's Ladder* was praised highly "Excellent Direction, fine change of dynamic lead to a superb finish."

❖ ❖ ❖

In 1990 the Choir made its first capital purchase apart from music, a Yamaha 'Clavinova'. The Choir had received a generous bequest six years earlier from the President's late mother, Mrs. Connie Gill, and in 1985 the members at the A.G.M. decided that this would form the basis of a fund to purchase the instrument. David Gill had agreed to add a further £50 or £75 to this figure if the cost of a piano was in the region of £150 to £175. The Conductor and Treasurer were authorised to follow up this matter.

However, we read nothing further until the A.G.M. of 1986, when it was stated that an electronic keyboard was still being sought. Nothing else is heard of the matter, but then in 1988, Richard Sibley and his working party were thanked for the production of new music folders, which had been first used at the Highbridge Festival. The net cost, it was reported, after Hammett's generous contribution, was more than covered by Connie Gill's bequest.

Eventually a Special Committee Meeting approved the purchase of what was described as a Yamaha electric organ at a cost of £1019. It would be available to the Reg Griffiths Singers, (the Afternoon Group) and other groups (unspecified) who would make a donation (also unspecified) to Choir funds. Although many members had misgivings about spending so much on property for the Choir, the instrument proved invaluable in enabling the choir to sing at venues where the piano was inadequate, or, increasingly, entirely missing.

The Choir Committee Minutes record that the Choir had first discussed the doubtful quality of pianos and hence the suitability of various venues for singing in June 1956, but the Committee agreed they would do the best they could despite the circumstances. However, now the Choir frequently found that many venues were without a piano or possessed one that could best be described as 'doubtful'.

A recent performance in the chapel of one of the public schools in the area revealed the fact that there was no instrument, so the Vice-Chairman had to be sent back to Taunton post haste to retrieve the Clavinova so the concert could go ahead. This illustrated the wisdom of the Conductor's insistence that the choir should be at a venue at least an hour beforehand to sort out these stage management problems.

As a result of a generous legacy from the late Reg Griffiths the purchase of a second, smaller and more portable instrument for the use of the Afternoon Group was authorised in June 1994, and with the Choir's customary speed, was bought in December 1996 for £249.

The Electric Organ became notorious on a choir outing to Middlezoy Methodist Church. Geoff Ede was responsible for delivering the instrument to the church but got lost. The choir made do with the church organ until in the middle of a song the doors of the church opened with a crash to reveal Geoff Ede who proceeded to explain his problem finding the church in a loud voice!

6 WITH A VOICE OF SINGING

The period from 1991 to 2005 was a pivotal period in the choir's development. Francis Burroughes joined the choir as its Musical Director in 1992 and remained in that position until 2006; his influence on the choir cannot be underestimated. Along with the return of Valerie Hill and the appointment of Hazel Reed as Accompanist in 1994 there was a new dawn in the choir's development which we will experience in later chapters.

The year 1991 was pivotal in another way. Jeff Tottle, the choir's very first conductor, died in May of that year. His memory lives on not only in the choir's memory but also through his son's marriage to Cyril Salway's daughter Carol. Later in this same period Cyril Salway passed away in 1997. In 2002 it was recorded that the choir had sung at the funeral of nine members in the preceding 18 months.

In May 1992 and 1993 the Choir travelled to Cardiff to sing in Cardiff Arms Park Stadium for another massed choir event, organised by the 'World Choir' organisation. The soloists on these occasions were Dame Gwynneth Jones, Tom Jones, Dennis O'Neill and Shirley Bassey.

There was an attempt to travel to Atlanta, U.S.A., in the early nineties to take part in yet another massed choir event, through an organisation known as 'The World Choir', but despite a successful event held four years earlier in South Africa (which our Choir did not attend), this time the organisation of the event was fraught with difficulties, such that many Choirs withdrew their support, and the World Choir organisation went into receivership. This experience made it extremely difficult for some years to persuade the Committee to embark on any scheme which involved the outlay of any funds. The counter-argument would always be "What about Atlanta?" or, to really ensure any project was still-born, "It will turn out to be another Atlanta."

Taunton Deane MVC organised two Massed Choir Galas, in 1996 and in 2000 and attended further ones in Swindon and Bournemouth, organised by local Male Voice Choirs, celebrating their own Jubilees. The format of the concerts remained the same; groups of massed choir items, interspersed with a soloist.

The choir in 1996 was made up of 50 singers as recorded in the pages of the County Gazette. Keen eyed observers will note that one singer from the very original Wessex Male Singers (Cyril Salway) was still singing with the choir 50 years on...also that a number of the singers are still with the choir in 2021.

PRESENT MEMBERS
of the Taunton Deane
Male Voice Choir 1996

First Tenor
IDRIS ARNDELL
ROY DAVIDSON
TONY OSMOND
LEN SEBRIGHT
LOUIS SHORNEY
TED WAY
GEOFF PICKERSGILL
STEPHEN BROTHERTON

Second Tenor
DENNIS ATTRILL
JOHN BIRD
GILBERT FAIRS
STUART GIFFORD
CYRIL SALWAY
DICK WILLIAMS
JOHN THOMAS
JOHN WILLIS
ALEC KENNEDY
DAI HELPS
MAURICE DAY
BRYN BEWICK

First Bass
REG ARBERRY
BRIAN ANDREWS
JOHN BLACKMORE
GEOFF EDE
ERIC HAYWARD
ALAN KIMBER
HAROLD PACKINGTON
BRIAN REYNOLDS
ALAN RICHARDS
DAVID SPEIGHT
BILL TAYLOR
TONY WEST
TONY WOOD
PAUL ZEAL
MICHAEL LEIGH
TONY SLAVIN

Second Bass
TREVOR DOWN
ROD CORKETT
TREVOR DAVIES
WYN DAVIES
GWYN FOSTER
REG GRIFFITHS
MAURICE HALLMARK
BILL HONEYMAN
CHARLES JOHNSTONE
BILL LEWIS
RON TROUP
MIKE WARD
BRIAN WALTERS
CYRIL VIAN
GRAHAM POPE

The 1996 Massed Choir Gala was part of TDMVC's Golden Jubilee celebrations, and was held in St. George's Hall, Exeter, there being no public hall available in Taunton big enough to house such an event. The Committee had considerable misgivings about the financial risk involved but, in the end, six choirs attended, with a total of about 400 singers taking part, and when all expenses had been paid at the end, a profit of just under a hundred pounds accrued to the choir.

The second gala in 2000 was held in Wells Cathedral. Eight Choirs took part with about 450 singers and over £2000 was raised for the Cathedral's Development Appeal.

The Choir also travelled to Hyde Park to take part in the Fiftieth V.E. Day Celebrations in May 1995 to sing as part of a massed Male Voice Choir. The soloists were Elaine Page, Cliff Richard, and Dame Vera Lynn, with narrations by Dorothy Tutin, Wendy Craig, Hannah Gordon, Honor Blackman and a host of other stars - an inspiring and memorable occasion.

John Blackmore, the Concert Secretary, spoke of the Hyde Park Concert at the AGM in 1995 when he said "Taking part in a national event of such significance was a wonderful experience, and something all those who went will be able to say to families and friends for years to come, 'I was there!' "

From 1996 the Choir became a little more adventurous, travelling to Manchester in March 2000 for a weekend to sing at the Male Voice Millennium Extravaganza at the Manchester Evening News Arena in aid of Help the Hospices and St. Anne's Hospice Greater Manchester. The soloists were Marie McLaughlin, soprano, the popular organist Nigel Ogde, and the Manchester Camerata Chamber Orchestra.

The music sung by the massed choirs included Welsh hymns, (*Llanfair, Gwahoddiad*, and *Tydi a Roddaist*) *The Pilgrims' Chorus* by Wagner, *Battle Hymn of the Republic*, and *You'll Never walk Alone, When the Saints go Marching In, The Lost Chord* and *Morte Criste*. Many members enjoyed an 'Afterglow' back at the hotel with other Choirs well into the small hours of the morning.

Another weekend excursion took place in London in November 2003 to sing with the Yorkshire Association of Male Voice Choirs in the Royal Albert Hall with a mixed choir of over 2000 participants, accompanied by two Brass Bands. It proved to be a major highlight in the history of the choir to which we will return.. The members singing in the Festival had to attend extra practices during July and August in order to learn the music, so for this year the customary Workshops were discontinued. The Conductor of the event travelled to Taunton with his assistant conductor and a soloist in order to take the Choir through the programme. Despite some trepidation the Choir survived the test.

The whole weekend was a tremendous success from the group meal in Islington on Friday, to the rehearsal and performance on Saturday and the mass community singing in Covent Garden on Sunday morning. The performance raised over £100,000 for Cancer Research U.K. The Choir repeated the experience with equal delight in November 2006.

Trevor Davies, Bass, recalls these events and more.

"Although the precise date is lost in the mists of time, I must have joined the choir in late 1993 or early 1994. I know this because my first big gig was a massed choir concert to celebrate the Swindon MVC 75th anniversary in 1994. It was held in in a large sports centre with perhaps 300 choristers, a military band and the usual clutch of bigwigs. The highlight was supposed to be the grand entrance of the massed choirs sweeping in pairs through the entrance doors at the rear of the hall with indoor fireworks and the band playing an overture. Timing was of the essence and choristers were lined up in pairs snaking right round the building like coiled springs waiting for the grand entrance. All went well in rehearsal, but come the big night, some overzealous clot had locked the doors preventing entry. On hearing the band, the choristers surged forward only to end up in a melee behind the locked doors while stewards ran about like headless chickens trying to find the key. Eventually, after about 2 repeats from the band and the fireworks just glowing embers we got in through a pall of smoke. I could barely stand or sing for laughing. I think the rest of the concert was a success.

It was an early introduction to the fact that MVC choristers have a bottomless ability to mess things up especially where (the dreaded word) movement is involved.

"When I joined then, as now, the basses were the strongest section by a country mile (Editor's note – as a Bass myself I would not question Trevor's comments but I suspect other voices might feel the same about their section...). Despite my inexperience I was immediately 'promoted' to the back row, in those days the preserve of senior choristers. Not because I was any good of course, but rather because no-one else would have seen the conductor if I had been put in the front row – not that they ever looked.

"There were a number of short chaps in the front row, including one who had the unnerving habit of turning round and glaring at those behind if he perceived a wrong note or phrase. He seemed to know every note and word perfectly – or at least we thought he did because we never actually heard him. Some christened him the 'Silent Bass'.

"In the back row, I had the choir chairman Wynn Davies on my right and Reg Griffiths on my left. Wynn taught me everything I know including (I later realised) a few wrong notes because 'he had always sung it that way'. For such an experienced chorister, he was surprisingly nervous immediately before a concert usually disappearing into the dark for a few drags on a cigarette somewhere out of sight as he wasn't supposed to smoke. But he was a good friend and companion and we supported each other through numerous local concerts. In those days we always seemed to end up in a pub afterwards. Reg Griffiths was a very good chorister and a true basso profundo with a huge voice that could drown out most of the choir. He had a mischievous (or awkward) sense of humour depending on your point of view.

"The choir was invited to attend a massed choir concert in celebration of the Millennium at the MEN Arena in Manchester. I think it was called '2000 for 2000' with the aim of getting 2000 singers. In the event I think they were a bit short of that number but it was a big concert supported by the Manchester Youth Orchestra. My over-riding memory is not the concert but the hotel.

"The choir had booked into the Britannia, a large city centre hotel where I had stayed previously on business with the Civil Service, and had ended up with a room with no windows. To prevent this happening again I had booked a premium room for Pam and I. The room turned out to be fine but, unfortunately, on the second night we found out we were in the midst of a Rastafarian wedding party who were charging about up and down our corridor until about 5 o'clock in the morning keeping us awake.

"The next significant concert I can remember is the VE Day 60th Anniversary Concert in Hyde Park. I am sure others will have more accurate recollections than I. But I do recall that the choir was supposed to be 3000 strong, there was a large military band and Cliff Richard and Elaine Page the stars plus a German lady – we were inclusive even then – who irritated everyone by disappearing into her caravan whenever there was some glitch, thereby keeping everyone waiting. A Welsh tenor started up 'why are we waiting' that was gradually taken up by the rest of the choir until we all were 'shushed' by an embarrassed BBC luvvie.

"Both Cliff Richard and Elaine Page were very natural, just patiently sitting in their seats during the inevitable rehearsal delays. When Elaine Page was introduced, she jumped up to the microphone waggled her bum and immediately had 3000 men in the palm of her hand – or did we imagine it was the other way round? The stage was so big that (as usual) the basses were relegated to a distant corner and had to watch the conductor on a TV monitor. During the rehearsal, whilst the band were playing the *Spitfire Fugue,* a Spitfire barrel rolled over Hyde Park – a real hairs on the back of the neck moment.

"As the concert approached, I recall some of our older members pinning on their medals - some for gallantry. It was a reminder that they were young once and were called upon to do and see things that we younger members will never (hopefully) have to endure. The evening crowd was vast, disappearing to infinity in the gloom with searchlights playing over it. At the end of the concert the principals and the conductor stood at the stage exits shaking hands with the choristers as they left. I got the conductor but David Speight got a peck on the cheek from Elaine Page. It was rumoured that he didn't wash for a week!

"Later, there are the Festival of Brass and Voices concerts in the Royal Albert Hall for Cancer Research. I think this originated amongst the many Yorkshire choirs but eventually they cast their net more widely and we were invited to attend. I have done 6 consecutively, so that makes my first in 2003 and the last in 2018. The format has always been the same with individual choir rehearsals, then a couple of larger 'area' rehearsals often with one of the bands, in our case usually at the Swindon Railway museum and then finally a long rehearsal in the Royal Albert Hall on the morning of the concert with both brass bands. No music of course and quite a lot of new material makes it a big ask but one that has always been hugely rewarding. Bill Relton used to be ably supported by a proper Yorkshireman - who took the role of chorus master. He used to wander round the sections during rehearsals bawling out wrong notes and poor preparation. But he was very good company later on in the bar.

"The RAH rehearsals were marathons lasting from about 9.30 for registration until mid-afternoon or when Bill thought we were ready for the concert. We were not allowed to leave and refreshment opportunities inside were very limited. Perversely, the only group allowed to leave were smokers who of course had to be indulged. Despite being a lifelong non-smoker, I used to take advantage of this loophole, by leading a posse of 'smokers' out of the building and into the Imperial College Union bar just few yards away for those in the know. This generally worked well, but on one occasion the college cash machine swallowed my card leaving me penniless in central London.

"Last time we went, I took Steve 'His Reverence' Reed but they were not impressed by my 1966 membership card and we got thrown out. The other thing about both rehearsals and concerts, although perhaps it was just me, was that 'bladder control' turned out to be an important quality for choristers. We had to be in our seats at 6.30 pm, an hour before the concert started with little opportunity to get to the loo until the end of the concert. I suspect there were many crossed legs.

"In the early days, all the choirs were Male Voices and the concerts were fronted by various hosts – David Jacobs, Frank Thornton (Captain Peacock) and (I think) Peter Sallis. But to my mind, it is the Brass Bands, invariably amongst the very best in the world, that made the concerts so special. One brass band at that level is great but 2 is just mind blowing. The volume and quality of sound when all the choristers were singing, both bands playing and the RAH organ joining in was literally earth moving – more 'hairs on the back of the neck' stuff. My favourite band piece - usually involving the Brighouse and Rastrick (as it is one of their party pieces) was *Elsa's Procession to the Cathedral* by Richard Wagner. They played it on 3 occasions. The sound just builds and builds until you think it just can't get any bigger, but it does and it ends with the bass drums on their side being played like timpani and the tuba players almost collapsing through exertion. Wonderful. Then there was the time we were rehearsing the *1812* and experimenting with the sound of the cannon – electronic unfortunately. Bill kept asking the choir whether it was loud enough, 'louder' they cried in reply until, on the final test – a huge blast - little bits of paint were observed falling from the RAH ceiling. It was turned down a notch or two for concert unfortunately.

"Of all the choral pieces my favourite has to be Gounod's *By Babylon's Wave* – an absolute pig to rehearse with a small choir but unbelievably powerful in performance opposite 300 or 400 tenors on top of their game – an unusual sight for us but nonetheless unforgettable.

"For our first outing we stayed in the Islington Hilton (the best hotel of the lot). On our first night there, whilst most of the party went into a restaurant next to the hotel, Pam and I ventured out with Rob and Mary Morgan to sample the delights of Islington nightlife. After a curry and a bit of a pub crawl down the High Street we ended up in The Kings Head Theatre Pub – a Young's pub - where, to their discomfort, the ladies attracted the attention of the pub drunkard leaving Rob and I time to sup a few pints of Young's best. When we got back to the hotel the rest of the choir were still back in the restaurant trying to sort out the bill. Table for 50 is never a good idea!

"For the next concert we stayed in Kensington at the old Kensington Close Hotel by then getting a bit run down. Pam and I had to change room three times but apart from that it was ideal because it was an easy taxi run to Knightsbridge for the museums and shopping, and better still we were able to walk back to the hotel after the concert without the usual interminable queuing. We found a little Italian restaurant in Kensington Church Street still open and all the usual suspects piled in there.

"Thereafter the choir took the cheaper option and stayed on the Heathrow corridor, firstly at the Park Hotel, and on the last 3 occasions at the St. Giles Hotel in Feltham. The downside of this arrangement was that there was a lot of bussing around to and from the rehearsal and concert. I didn't like it, and usually stayed up in town changing into my concert kit in either the Mormon Church basement (don't ask) or Science Museum cloakroom.

"At the Park we were lucky enough to stay with the Scottish Fiddlers – one of the acts in the concerts – who put on an impromptu show. I also recall one of our (ahem) senior members – without wishing to identify him - a former padre – throwing his car keys into the ring of guests and daring any lady to get up and dance with him. It was my wife Pam who took up the challenge! Although a bit quirky the St Giles turned out to be ideal socially. There was a Weatherspoon's pub just down the road which most gravitated to where you could get a pint of Doom Bar for £1.99 – cheaper than in Taunton. It was there that we listened in horror to the developing outrage at the Bataclan in Paris. It had implications for us all the following day, as we were held outside the RAH for hours in cold and rain whilst the building was searched. The rehearsal had to be significantly curtailed. Most of the concert organisers also stayed at the St Giles so the after-glow afterwards was usually superb.

"Finally, a word about one of the early choir tours. You will hear from others about the memorable trips to Lisieux and Rotterdam, but I suspect not many are left who went to Jersey for an International Festival. Pam and I flew out and extended the trip with a stay at a top hotel, but the others went by ferry and had to endure a very rough crossing. We joined up with Francis Burroughes' other choir – Trinity Opera – for this trip, as both were short in some sections so, to make the numbers work, some of us doubled up by singing in both choirs. I was one of those in both choirs. This resulted in some chaotic travel arrangements with us dashing around the island by bus from one venue to another with the '2 choirs choristers' having to change in the bus en route. This led to the unfor-tunate image of Francis the MD careering down the isle of the bus in his union jack underpants with his trousers round his ankles when the bus lurched and braked suddenly. The ladies didn't know where to look.

"Another incident occurred very late at night when the hotel management decided that a massed rendition of *Nessun Dorma* was not appropriate. One of our (then) younger members was led astray by a senior chorister who took him out for a 'few beers'. The next morning our young friend was 'hors de combat' and unfit to attend rehearsal. Pam was left in charge of him at breakfast, she distinctly remembers him putting a small box of cornflakes into a cereal bowl and then pouring milk over the lot - box and all. No wonder he found it a bit chewy. As for the singing, well the MVC were unplaced, but Trinity Opera got through to the final in the huge International Arena – one of the most daunting stages I have ever sung on. The winners were a group of university students from Eastern Europe studying voice, so were of a professional standard."

John Blackmore remembers VE day 1995 well. He recalls the day dawned bright and gently warm with a few light clouds. "We gathered. 1,000 men from around the United Kingdon...we were ready!

"In Hyde Park a huge outdoor stage had been prepared with a Dove of Peace hung at the front. One thousand male choristers from various male voice choirs across the nation, including our very own Taunton Deane Male Voice Choir, ready under the baton of Owain Arwel Hughes, mounted the steeply raked seating at the back of the stage to face an audience estimated at around 100,000 people. We looked good in our light blue shirts and dark trousers!

"Royalty were present with Her Majesty the Queen, Prince Philip, Prince Charles, Princess Diana and the two young Princes William and Harry.

"We weren't alone of course. All the great and the good of entertainment were there – Dame Vera Lynn (of course), Cliff Richard, Elaine Paige, Michael Elphick, and a Russian bass who sang *Kalinka* backed by the male voice choir. Many others too numerous to recall.

"The atmosphere was quite wonderful. Everyone was enjoying themselves. Then came our solo slot! The massed choir sang a medley of wartime songs – *Roll out the Barrel*, *Bless them All* and several others. Down front dancers dressed as pearly kings and queens were doing a soft shoe shuffle. But then the audience started to cheer wildly and wave their flags. Well, I thought, we are good but not THAT good!

"There was a rumble which rapidly grew to a roar and out from over our heads and across the park flew three aircraft from the Memorial Flight. A majestic Lancaster flanked by a Hurricane and a Spitfire! We didn't mind being upstaged by those three!

"After Dame Vera had led the whole cast in a rendition of *We'll Meet Again* we trooped off the stage back through the Performers area which was already largely empty. But as we threaded our way through the seating and barriers to head back to our coach we spotted one lone performer sat taking in the atmosphere and relaxing. It was the lovely Elaine Paige. And she had the grace to talk with us choristers and thank US for our contribution to the concert. What a classy lady!

It was in 2004 that Evan Williams joined the choir.

"Lesley persuaded me that I should attend the TDMVC annual concert. When the choir mounted the stage I was pleasantly surprised to find that there were many familiar faces. I really enjoyed the concert and we went to the afterglow with a dear friend, Tony Osmond, and his wife Barbara. I gave in to Tony's persuasive chat and made one of the best decisions of my life - I joined the choir.

"There have followed seventeen years of sheer pleasure. Singing in hundreds of venues from cathedrals, churches, theatres, the Royal Albert Hall and the Eden Project, to name just a few.

"But two occasions really stand out in my memory. The first was the tour to Taunton's twin town of Lisieux. The second occasion was the weekend tour to Amsterdam. (editor – we will return to these events and Evan's memories in Chapter 7)

"Thank you Taunton Deane Male Voice Choir for giving me some of the happiest days of my life. Congratulations on your 75th anniversary and here's to many more successful years."

VOICE-MALE

In the autumn of 1994, John Blackmore produced the first edition of the Choir's Newsletter. John had joined the Committee in December 1992 in the newly created post of Concert Secretary, to which he added a Publicity role. The first edition was a two-sided sheet, and included short articles and notices by Francis Burroughes, David Gill, Wynn Davies, Geoff Ede, Brian Reynolds, and Reg Griffiths. It was so well received that John volunteered to produce another newsletter before the end of the season. On the 15 of May 1995, newsletter number two was produced, with articles by Wynn Davies, Francis Burroughes, and Reg. Griffiths. The publication continued to be biannual under the editorship of Tony West from 1996.

Tony Slavin took over as Editor when he became Concert secretary in 2001 and introduced the title Voice-Male in December 2001. At first appearing twice yearly, it generally appeared more frequently, and has at times expanded from one or two A4 pages to a 16 or 20 page magazine. Usually there were articles from the Choir President, Chairman, and Conductor, news and reports of concerts and social events, and very often contributions from members about their own interests and hobbies.

John Crosby took over as editor in 2006, relieving chairman, Tony Slavin, of one of his many responsibilities. Voice-Male is a hugely valuable resource and has been drawn on many times for this history. The original copies will be accessible in the choir's archive at the Somerset Heritage Centre along with much fascinating material and artefacts.

The Choir used to have a 'laissez-faire' attitude to recruiting. In 1987 one of the most positive actions that it took was to authorise Dennis Attrill, Geoff

Ede, and Richard Sibley to design a postcard inviting men to join the Choir. The card could be displayed in prominent places such as Libraries and Community Centres. As a result of these three members' labour, one card at least was displayed in Taunton Library, where it remained on view until 1994.

In February 1999 the Conductor organised a large display in the entrance of the new Taunton Library, and members were encouraged to 'man the stall' in uniform whenever they had an hour to spare, to hand out leaflets, and publicise the Choir. This attracted so much interest that the effort was repeated in August and September for the beginning of the next season, and became an annual event for the next three or four years. (Maybe we can consider doing this again??? - Editor)

One other very long-term idea was to start a Junior Male Voice Choir, for which the Committee set aside some £200 in case it should get off the ground and some 'seed-corn' funds were needed. After a great deal of effort, and visiting of schools and publicity, about half a dozen boys were recruited, all from one school, and although the boys were keen, the Conductor felt that he could not justify the effort to continue with the scheme, and so regretfully it ceased after one term, and the £200 returned to Choir funds.

Jack Dennis

If it were not for Jack Dennis much of this book would be blank pages. As editor I have been able to draw on a veritable treasure trove of material Jack so diligently researched, recorded and presented. Here he tells us how and when he joined the choir and later thoughts.

"I first knew of the choir in the mid 1990s I guess when David Speight pestered me to join but I was not really keen at the time. Alf Anstee had also been trying to get me to join at this time and at Christmas time 1998 he told me he would pick me up and take me with him to the first rehearsal after Christmas. I do not think either of them had heard me sing but others had who had tried to get me to join the RiverTones*. At University in Sheffield I had sung various lead roles in G&S productions and one or two thought I should consider training to become a singer (do not laugh) but I thought they were mad! I was firmly committed to teaching (thankfully).

"I joined the choir in January 1999 and was not keen at first but the fun and camaraderie soon had me hooked and I have always loved being in the choir. I know that others have no idea when they joined (Alf for example) but I have all the original registers in my possession and can find all the correct joining details without too much bother. As I keep saying to Richard Salter (*Secretary*) 'record is better then recollection' but not everybody agrees!

"Sadly I am not enjoying this period in the choir due to lockdown. I am not enjoying the Zooms and can not really follow what Nick Thomas, MD, is doing on screen, what he wants, what we are singing, where we are in the song etc etc."

*Jack Dennis mentions being persuaded to join RiverTones, and this history would not be complete without recognising the other major Male singing group in Taunton. RiverTones are an acapella barbershop choir with over 50 members and have a high reputation which is justly deserved. There is a little overlap between the two choirs, with at any time a small number of men singing with both choirs.

7 THE PERFECT MALE VOICE CHOIR

60th Anniversary Year

Flushed with success from singing from memory for the first time at the Annual Concert in 2005 the choir rushed into 2006 with great enthusiasm, and a choir membership of over 50.

There were 3 editions of Voice-Male published in 2006, which was the choir's Diamond Jubilee Year. They were definitely needed just to record the wide range of activities and events of the Diamond Jubilee.

The first major event was the Celebration Dinner held at Taunton and Pickeridge Golf Club. 109 people attended with only 2 people crying off due to sickness. Voice-Male reported that the occasion was so obviously successful in cementing the comradeship and social bonding that is now such a strong feature of our choir.

John Crosby and Brian Reynolds received special thanks for the efforts they put into the organisation of the event. It was considered that the evening of good fellowship, gentle imbibing and enjoyable banter would surely remain a permanent memory of the Diamond Jubilee Year. Similar events have been held since 2006 with similar success.

Our President David Gill was presented with an inscribed cut-glass bowl in recognition of his 25 years unstinting service and support of the choir.

John Crosby made a presentation of a "Papal" certificate conferring 'Sainthood' on our Musical Director Dr Francis Burroughes.

Jack Dennis led the Afterglow group who serenaded the diners, or attempted to because most were unable to read their songbooks in the dim lighting (another good reason for singing without copy!)

Quiz wizards Trevor and Pam Davies devised a quiz that succeeded in baffling most of us but there were actually several winners and there needed to be a draw to decide on who got which prize. Paddy O'Boyle organised a raffle of prizes donated by members and the proceeds boosted Choir Funds.

There have been a number of excellent choir dinners since 2006, but this a wonderful occasion and worth lingering over. It is notable that so many of the key organisors in 2006 are still active and with us today except for Brian Reynolds who died in 2018 and John Crosby who we lost in 2021.

2007 opened with the choir singing at St Michael's Galmington and we were joined by soloist Mary Morgan. Jeff Davies wrote for Voice-Male, and paid homage to his favourite soprano:

"I first saw and heard Mary sing at St. Michael's Church Galmington last January and was most impressed by the quality of her performance, and amazed that such a talented professional should be singing with us amateurs in a suburban church on a cold Saturday night. As her renderings progressed it became clear that her innate charm and modesty and complete lack of a diva's histrionics rapidly formed a mutual bond between her and her audience.

"I was therefore delighted to learn that Mary was going to join us for our concert at St. John's Wellington and that she was going to repeat Purcell's *Music for a While* as well as Gounod's *Ave Maria* which she had delivered sublimely to a most appreciative audience at St. Michael's.

"However, it was *Music for a While* that interested me most for, many years ago, as an aspiring young baritone my singing teacher at Birmingham School of Music, Linda Vaughan, entered me into a competition and chose *Music for a While* as my entry piece.

"I practised assiduously, aware of how technically difficult the music is, and that perfect pitch was necessary at all time. My big night arrived and nervous and tense (the former understandable, the latter a bane to singers) I delivered Purcell's classic to less than ecstatic applause. Unlike the 'X' Factor where the judges verbally confront the contestants immediately we had to wait until the end of the competition for the batting order to be announced and we were handed a written appraisal of our performance. I will not bore you with the details, but after all these years, I can still remember the judge's chastening remarks about my lack of interpretation of the mood of the music.

"Not so with Mary, who gave a superbly controlled performance with minimal vibrato, particularly in the sotto voce passages, and showed her technical excellence and versatility throughout the concert, concluding with Eric Coates' *I Heard You Singing*. The applause from the large audience was long and heart felt.

"I have since heard down the grapevine that Mary has been singing in Europe. I am not at all surprised that her talent is being recognised afar and that Galmington and Wellington are but temporary horizons. I doubt if Mary has a marketing agent as she appears far too self-effacing. She does not need one. Word of mouth is a powerful publicity machine. Her voice will do the talking."

The editor at the time of Voice-Male commented that Mary has performed with Taunton Deane MVC on several occasions and is regarded by many in the choir as their favourite soloist. She has taught music at Wells Cathedral School, Queens College and Bridgwater College and has performed major classical works with various choral societies more distinguished than our own. She is married to a member of our choir, first bass Rob Morgan, leaving other members consumed with jealousy. Long may she sing.

Now in 2021 we all look forward to Mary singing with us again at our 75th anniversary concert at St Andrews Rowbarton.

Royal Albert Hall

Every three years since 2003 our choir has participated in the Festival of Brass and Voices at the Albert Hall. Each concert has been a huge fund raiser for Cancer Research, in fact the biggest in the country. The participation size of our choir has increased over the years. Singing with 1500 others and two of the best brass bands in the country has been quite unbelievable, another incredible singing experience as a member of our choir.

Male and female choirs come from all over the country and the brass bands have included The Brighouse and Rastrick from Yorkshire, The Cory Band from South Wales and The Grimethorpe Colliery Band also from Yorkshire. We have filled the Albert Hall with wonderful, classic pieces including *The Halleluiah Chorus* , *Gloria*, *By Babylon's Wave*, *Goin' Home*, *With a Voice of Singing*, *Gwahoddiad* and *Morte Christe*.

Our preparation had been extremely thorough with local rehearsals being led by Val Hill and later by Nick Thomas. These have always been followed by a regional rehearsal of southern choirs at the Steam museum in Swindon and a final morning rehearsal in the Albert Hall on the day of the concert. Every performance has been conducted by the incomparable Bill Relton whose musical CV is outstanding, including principal trumpet at Sadler's Wells Opera and the BBC concert orchestra.

It was an honour to persuade Bill to come and speak at our choir dinner in 2016. Bill's address was interesting and inevitably amusing. He, of course, wore his trademark red braces and many of our choir showed our appreciation for his dress when they divested their dinner jackets to reveal many pairs of red braces! It is hoped that Bill is sprightly enough in his early nineties to conduct the postponed 2021 concert in 2023! The 2021 festival was postponed due to the Covid 19 virus that swept the country in 2020.

Lisieux

In May 2016 the choir embarked on its first overseas tour, to Lisieux, which is Taunton's French twin town. From Steve and Hazel Reed's association with the twinning group the links were made with Patrick Buhot, who was the excellent leader of the group on the other side of the channel. Literally hundreds of emails were exchanged and many phone calls made between Steve and Patrick in the year leading up to the trip. Three choir members - John Capell (Chairman), Tony Moore (Concert Secretary) and Steve Reed (Social Secretary) made a recce visit to ensure that all concert venues were viewed, the itinerary finalised and the red wine sampled.

And so, on 13th May the choir assembled at 5am to leave for Poole and the ferry to Cherbourg. Many of the group were hosted, making attempts to improve their French, whereas others stayed in the Grand Hotel de L'Esperance. The whole party was welcomed with drinks and pastries before dispersing to homes and the hotel.

On the Saturday morning there was a local market before a welcome reception at the Town Hall with the Mayor (Monsieur Bernard Aubril). And more coffee and pastries for the whole party. Presentations were made and speeches given, Chairman John Capell trying hard to present his in the best possible French.

There followed a trip to Chateau Musee de Saint German de Livet and its lovely gardens; then back to Lisieux to the Basilica St Therese, looking over the town and said to be one of the greatest churches of the 20th Century. Some visited the crypt, some preferred to head off to fill the nearby cafes! A lot of long and late lunches and time spent in Lisieux - then in the evening out into the countryside to the pretty village of Moyaux for an excellent concert.

The solo pieces were sung by Mary Morgan and were especially well-received, particularly the Mozart, *Laudate Dominum* and *Ave Maria*. This was a memorable evening (and not just because of the ambulance for Tony Waite! Fortunately, he made a good recovery to re-join the party next day).

(ed: Tony Waite performed a vital role for the choir as Risk Officer preparing Risk Assessments to ensure Choir and audience were safe - he still provides this service even though he is not singing with the choir at present)

On Sunday we travelled by coach to Honfleur, to follow Patrick around the streets and alleyways to the museum seeing many decorated boats; also the church and fountain. People then wandered the shops and enjoyed the lovely harbour, before moving on to Chateau du Breuil, Calvados distillery, where picnics were enjoyed in the woodlands before a tour and sampling!

After a very relaxed and sunny day, back to Lisieux to prepare for the evening concert. This was an excellent performance despite difficult acoustics. There followed a Grand Dinner at the hotel with excellent food, presented with crossed flags on each table and a great atmosphere. The menu included rabbit terrine, guinea fowl in cider sauce and more all served with more wine which saw us through the entertaining speeches and afterglow performances.

On the final day we left early following a fond and amusing farewell from Patrick. We headed for Pegasus Bridge for what was to be the most memorable and moving part of our trip. We received a detailed presentation about the brave pilots who risked everything to fly behind enemy lines in planes, carefully designed but extremely fragile, in order to be most effective in the circumstances.

After hearing stories of these brave 2nd world war pilots we sang *Requiem to a Soldier* from Band of Brothers and *You Raise Me Up.* John Capell recalls that this was one of the best singing moments ever. Our voices were affected by the presentation – the T2s begin the piece accompanying with 'Ahs', trying to accomplish that with voices tinged with emotion and pride was challenging.

We then went on to Arromanche and the Normandy beaches, where some of the group went off to eat while others visited the museum including a moving film of the landings. The final stop of our wonderful visit was at St Mere Eglise which is a quiet country town with another small museum memorialising their part in the war including the model of the parachuting soldier caught on the church tower. Many in the party ended the tour with an excellent local ice-cream!

John Capell, then Chairman, recalls "As a post script to the Lisieux trip, Patrick and his wife hosted three of our party, Ruth and I as well as Paull Robathan.

John spent a few worthwhile chats over a glass of wine or two persuading Paull that he should consider volunteering to be the next Chairman. Amazing what some good wine can do!!"

Evan Williams continues his recollections...."A fantastic weekend of singing and friendship was rounded off with a visit to the Normandy D-Day area. It culminated when we were given a guided tour of Pegasus Bridge that had been the scene of a brilliant action carried out by British airborne troops.

"Following a guided tour, we assembled in the large lobby of the museum and with Hazel on keyboard and Nick on flute, we gave our rendition of the moving *Requiem for a Soldier*. The singing was excellent and things were fine as people gathered in a good crowd. All was well until I noticed two elderly ladies to one side who were weeping. That was the end of my singing - I wonder what thoughts were running through their minds."

Armistice Concert

2018 marked 100 years since the Armistice in 1918 that ended the First World War. On Saturday 27th October St Mary Magdalene Church in Taunton was almost over flowing with people, filled to capacity for an event - much more than a concert - to commemorate and reflect on those who served in the Great War, but also service men and women who have given their all through the decades.

Pauline Homeshaw of FOSS (Friends of Somerset SSAFA the Armed Forces Charity, the Soldiers, Sailors, Airmen and Families Association) recalls the evening.

"Taunton Deane Male Voice Choir, the Taunton Military Wives Choir and the Royal Air Force Association Concert Band performed a poignant and yet stirring concert to mark the Armistice in 1918.

"Poignant, stirring and thoughtful music and words made the concert a perfect commemoration for the audience to absorb the thoughts and memories that so many families have with the Great War. The three musical elements of the evening balanced each other well and gave a fitting tribute to those who fought for our freedom.

"Special guests at the concert included Admiral of the Fleet Sir Benjamin Bathurst GCB DL and Lady Bathurst, Mayor of Taunton Deane Councillor Catherine Herbert and her Consort, Denis Burn Esq, High Sheriff of Somerset, Rebecca Powe MP and Mr Charles Clark, Air Marshall Sir Baz North KCB OBE MA and Lady North and Chairman of SSAFA Somerset, Rear Admiral Andrew Gough CB and Mrs Gough."

Nick Thomas, Musical Director of Taunton Deane Male Voice Choir, choreographed a moving opening spectacle that saw the choir split into four sections advancing from all corners of the church to the sound of gunfire and battle cries. The four groups were all singing different WW1 songs, combining as they reached the climax to sing in unison *I Want To Go Home*. The concert concluded with *The Last Post* played by trumpeter Matthew Osborne followed by *The National Anthem*.

The Afterglow was held at Somerset County Cricket Ground (see Chapter 11 for more about Afterglows). A large contingent combined to produce a fitting conclusion to a memorable evening.

It is appropriate to remember one attendee, Sam Smalldon, Sergeant at Mace to the Mayor of Taunton Deane. He is missed by so many. The Somerset County Gazette marked his untimely passing in 2019.

"Sam, who lived in Taunton, where he had been educated at Castle Secondary Modern School, was a former Royal Engineer who had served in Northern Ireland and the Falklands. He was a passionate supporter of veterans who had fallen on hard times and was delighted when homeless charity ARC opened Victoria House, a home for former troops living on the streets. He trained as a psychological first aider so he could spot the signs of 'vets' at risk of taking their own lives. He also managed the poppy appeal in Taunton."

Trip to Holland

as described by Rev Steve Reed

"The choir certainly gained a taste for international travel and just three years after visiting Lisieux in 2016 we made our second visit across the channel, this time to Holland in May 2019. Why choose Holland and how did the visit emerge? It was chorister Richard Venn who suggested the idea because of course English is very much the second language in that country. We emailed over 20 Dutch choirs offering a 'twinning' arrangement of visits in both directions. Three or four choirs responded of which two seemed favourites.

"During the summer of 2018 Steven & Hazel Reed, whilst on holiday in Holland, met with leaders from the two choirs and it immediately became clear that Mannenkoor "Prins Alexander" in Rotterdam was the most enthusiastic and a relationship was initiated. In early New Year 2019 Steve & Hazel together with the then choir Secretary Stuart Gifford (and wife Marianne) visited Rotterdam to cement the relationship, experience the Bastion Alexander Hotel and visit performance locations. Whilst the visit to Lisieux was on the back of an existing twinning relationship with Taunton, with choir members being hosted in private homes, quite early on we perceived that hosting was not sufficiently popular with the Dutch choir and thus a local hotel was selected. Thankfully the Dutch choir contact (Aad Van Der Wilt) a retired school teacher had excellent English and thus begun an almost daily stream of emails as the tour began to develop with much enthusiasm on both sides.

"And so it was, at 0500 on 9th May 2019 we boarded the luxury double decker Berrys coach bound for Holland for a long weekend. The party totalled 82, of which 50 choristers, some with accompanying wives, with a few choosing to take their cars in order to extend their stay on the continent. The trip out was not without its challenges. We arrived on time in Dover to find that the workers at the French port of Calais were holding a strike and the ferries remained idle. Whilst the delay was only a few hours we had a significant choice to make between *dinner or performance*. We had booked dinner at the Flanders Lodge hotel in the Belgian town of Ypres where we were to perform at the famous Menin

Gate.

"The Menin Gate Memorial to the Missing is a war memorial, dedicated to the British and Commonwealth soldiers who were killed in the Ypres Salient of World War I and whose graves are unknown. Following the Menin Gate Memorial opening in 1927, the citizens of Ypres wanted to express their gratitude towards those who had given their lives for Belgium's freedom. Hence every evening at 20:00, buglers from the Last Post Association close the road which passes under the memorial and sound the *"Last Post"* and visiting choirs may sing a couple of suitable songs. Running as late as we were the *eat or sing* decision had to be made. To a man we decided for singing and what a wise choice that was even though the financial loss to us was over a thousand euros as the hotel had already prepared the food. Those few who travelled by car ate very well at the hotel that day whilst the rest of us enjoyed ferry fodder!

"Although we were on a visit to Holland, all would agree that singing at the Menin Gate in Belgium was the most moving of experiences. We sang *Morte Christe* and *I have a Dream* ably conducted by accompanist Hazel Reed with our musical director Nick Thomas playing his accordion. The memory of Evan Williams wearing his military beret climbing steps (assisted by John Capell) to lay a wreath on behalf of the choir will be forever captured in the minds of many.

"We sang with a passion in a location which added to the quality of our singing and whilst there were hundreds present to watch the ceremony, silence followed our performance as clapping is forbidden, the focus rightly being upon the *lost*. Many came to thank the choir and some emailed phone videos of our performance. In the writer's opinion, had the trip finished there it would have all been worthwhile. We were in Ypres and Dutch hotel beds beckoned and thus we departed Belgium, a tired but contented group.

"A *PS* to the Ypres visit is that we had also planned to visit Essex Farm Cemetery. Here there is a memorial commemorating Lt Col John McCrae who famously wrote the poem *In Flanders Fields* which chorister John Blackmore was to have read. Sadly this too had to be abandoned.

"Thereafter the visit to Holland went very much to plan and our Dutch friends were most gracious and welcoming. Our 3 days based in the Prins Alexander suburb of Rotterdam were filled with getting to know the Dutch sights and sounds and singing with our new Dutch friends. The first morning we would either wander at leisure in Rotterdam centre or take a guided walking tour led by Gerry a Dutch choir member and qualified guide. Several of our party took advantage of a harbour Boat Trip to experience one of the world's largest ports in all its glory. In the afternoon we visited the Hillegondakerk the oldest church in Rotterdam. Here we sang a few songs, heard a short history of the place and enjoyed the inescapable cup of wonderful Dutch coffee which became a staple in all our visits.

"That evening we performed our main concert at the Alexanderkerk, the church which is home to our host choir. We benefited from an all too brief rehearsal of the two choirs of songs we were to sing together and then performed to a packed and appreciative audience. We are blessed to have an excellent soprano soloist who is wife to chorister Rob Morgan. Mary performed for us that evening and in the mind of many never sang better. Presents were exchanged but it is sad to report that our Chairman, Paull Robathan, was unable to make the trip because of ill health. However, the large picture of the Rotterdam skyline presented to Steven Reed by the Dutch choir now sits in the home of a grateful Chairman. Following a brilliant first day the not too weary gathered in the hotel bar for a traditional afterglow.

"Day 2 saw us in the historical and beautiful city of Delft, a canal-ringed city in the western Netherlands, which is known as the home of the world-famous Delftware, hand-painted blue-and-white pottery. The medieval Oude Kerk (Old Church) is the burial site of native son and Dutch Master painter Johannes Vermeer. After meeting up with Dutch friends for coffee and cake at the Hampshire Hotel, we wandered over to the Oude Kerk, taking in the sites on a pleasant Spring morning. Here we sang what appeared to be an impromptu concert to the many surprised but delighted tourists.

"Lunch and further Delft sightseeing were enjoyed before our coaches took us off to visit the incredible Maeslantkering which is a movable storm surge barrier spanning the New Waterway (Nieuwe Waterweg), a canal that connects the river Rhine to the North Sea. The Maeslantkering is a set of two swinging doors almost as long as the Eiffel tower and weighs about four times as much. It is the only storm surge barrier in the world with such large moveable parts. The

Maeslantkering acts as a final line of defence for Rotterdam against high levels of incoming seawater. It is one of largest moving structures on Earth.

"Our day concluded with a scenic drive along the Nieuwe Maas and Ijssel waterways and an evening social event at the Comenius college where we enjoyed an Old Dutch meal (stamppot buffet) and we provided glasses of Somerset cider for our hosts. Each choir had selected typical afterglow songs by which we entertained each other accompanied by Nick Thomas on the accordion. And so ended another full and pleasant day.

"Our final day mainly involved travel back to the UK but not before participating in the Sunday morning service at the Alexanderkerk with appropriate hymns from our Welsh repertoire (in English). The preacher was chorister Rev Steven Reed translated by the church's minister Rev. Robert-Jan van Amstel who also translated the prayers led by chorister David Corry. Inevitably there was coffee and cake following the service and many handshakes and farewells from our new-found Dutch friends whom we hope to see visiting Taunton in the future. The trip home was uneventful but we carried with us memories of a full, interesting and significant weekend.

"So with just two trips outside the UK in our 75 year history we certainly have some international 'catch up' to do and Covid willing we shall be planning another trip very soon."

Evan Williams continues his recollections ..

"The second occasion was the weekend tour to Amsterdam. An early start saw us well on the way to Dover where, after a very long delay which we learned was down to industrial action by the French civil service!, a good crossing was made to Calais.

"Next port of call was Ypres for the Last Post ceremony at the Menin Gate. Because we were running late the pre-planned meal at an hotel was skipped, choristers preferring to sing! After a very cold period of waiting, the choir performed superbly in front of the thousand or so spectators.

"Thanks to Steven Reed, and with assistance from John Capell, I had the great honour of representing the choir and, with Steve's blessing, my old regiment, the Grenadier Guards, by laying a wreath in memory of the many thousands of young men who made the ultimate sacrifice for all of us.

"It is a memory that I shall treasure forever."

◆ ◆ ◆

Chris Grabham

The choir was surprised, it is fair to say, when we were introduced to Chris Grabham in 2016. Still at school Chris turned out not only to be a charismatic and highly competent conductor, but was an immediate hit with the choir and has been with us on and off ever since.

"It was a cold, dark, winter's night in January 2016, when I first met the Taunton Deane Male Voice Choir. I remember being taken aback by the size of the choir; there must have been about 60 members present, but to my 17-year-old self they were the biggest choir that I had ever worked with. Strangely, I did not feel nervous, although I was a little apprehensive about how the choir may respond to me. As the rehearsal began, I sat beside Hazel Reed to page-turn, and eagerly awaited my time with 'the baton'.

"After a few warm-ups, and a fine rendition of *Let All Men Sing,* Nick Thomas introduced me to the choir and handed me *Anthem* for the first time. Little did I know that this piece would become one of my favourites, and it would be a song which I would conduct in numerous concerts across the South West. Whilst I must admit that I do not remember much of the music which occurred during our first meeting, I do fondly remember the welcome which the choir gave me. I knew that this would be the beginning of a fantastic partnership.

"It wasn't until February when I came across my favourite piece to conduct with the choir, Wagner's magnificent *Roman War Song* from the opera 'Rienzi'. *War Song* is a challenging piece in many aspects, requiring expert focus and military precision at times, but if these technical challenges can be correctly pulled off, it is a resounding success with our audiences. Indeed, throughout my 5 years in conducting the choir, this piece has been the most enjoyable (although *Gwahoddiad* does provide some competition in that respect!). Some stand-out performances of *War Song* which always spring to mind are: the concert at Launceston as part of the International Male Voice Choir Festival in 2017, and as part of our competitive performance in the Mid-Somerset Festival during March 2020, just days before the first nationwide COVID lockdown.

"Some of my favourite memories with the choir to date include: the tour to Cornwall in 2017 which, despite the awful weather, was the first time I had ever toured with any music group. We had a lot of fun during the tour, with plenty of fantastic music, and I really enjoyed spending time with the choir members in the evenings. Performing at the Eden Project during this tour was also a very poignant and memorable experience. I also fondly remember the Mayor's concert in October 2019, as this was the first concert in which I conducted TDMVC alone. It was a very exciting to lead the choir through so many contrasting pieces, all whilst raising money for charity.

"Working with a choir like Taunton has brought me so many fantastic opportunities and experiences, and I am so pleased that I have been able to share this journey with the choir. The choir's support throughout the years has been unwavering, and I feel privileged as a young person to be admitted into this mature club of very distinguished individuals. It has been a wonderful experience to work with Nick Thomas and Hazel Reed so closely over the years, and I have made many memories.

"Thank you to all of the choir members for your attention, encouragement and support over the past 5 years, and I look forward to continuing in the role of Assistant Musical Director for the foreseeable future."

Chris's latest performance with the choir was at the Mid Somerset Festival just as Covid-19 began its devastating invasion of our lives. On March 11th 2020 we received a message from the organisors "We would like to reassure everyone that we are currently planning to go ahead with the festival as there appears to be no Covid-19 infection concerns in the immediate area. It is however a rapidly evolving situation and we will continue to monitor it closely. Please check the website regularly."

That same evening the 22 members of our choir who had been rehearsing with Chris Grabham and accompanist Tom Morrell all committed to go to Bath for the competition on the 14th March. It is best for me to leave Jack Dennis to describe the day....

The Magnificent Seven + Twelve Go To Bath!

"The early train to Bath was no joke at 6.57am but Jeff Garland still managed to complain at having to get up so late. A quick rendition of *Farmer's Boy* soon cheered him though.

"When I finally found enough pound coins for the car park charge I arrived on the middle station to find the train already there and the three Furlong Green boys in the carriage enacting the Potsdam Conference of 1945. A few more choir members eventually arrived including Francis Lewis at 6.54. He seemed visibly upset when Duncan Hughes arrived at 6.55, looking very cool and urbane as usual.

"Poor Francis had temporarily lost his last to arrive gold medal but he took it very well in his usual amiable fashion. The cross country route took us through an amazing number of stations and seemed to find places that did not exist. However, we eventually arrived at Bath and made our way to the warm up venue.

"Things became much more lively when Chris Grabham arrived like the personification of *Puppet on a String* and began to lead us through our four songs in his usual brilliant, enthusiastic way. I think poor Brian Parkes was exhausted just watching him! Our first two songs went really well and we were given some excellent tips and an Agincourt-like call to vocal chords by Chris.

"We were the second of two male voice choirs in our section and I thought we sang really well. The contrast between *Roman War Song*, which shook the ceiling, and *The Rose* was especially good. Somehow the Adjudicator awarded the cup to the other choir by a single point,which surprised the members of other choirs present, who thought we were clearly better.

"The rehearsal of our other two songs did not go well so we aborted with Alf's usual comment that it would be alright on the night and wandered back to sing our second set of songs.

"The second class was Popular or Show Song and the competition was very strong with some really excellent well rehearsed and top quality groups. We were a bit concerned about Alf when we read that limited movement was acceptable in case he keeled over but he closed his eyes at the right place and survived when the Andover Ladies choir did a few moves. We all thought he had been very brave.

"Our rendition of *Tell My Father* was superb and I noticed some of the ladies crying at the end of the song. This came under the 'believe what you are singing' category when we really connected with the audience and got our message across. This is very difficult to achieve. Our singing of *Anthem* brought the house down and we received the longest and loudest ovation of the day which was very rewarding.

"We finished third out of six very high quality choirs which I thought was a great achievement. To put our achievement into context I should mention we were a scratch choir and had only rehearsed together on two occasions for about an hour and a half. The other choirs were experienced groups who obviously sing together very often and were very well rehearsed and drilled.

"Our real star was Chris Grabham who did a brilliant job leading, encouraging us and interpreting the music. I know we were all very impressed by his efforts and grateful for his hard work.

"The journey back was enlivened when I managed to lose my ticket and everybody on the train got involved in the search and people off other trains also pitched in. My good friend Alf even searched my wallet and was not put off at the moths which escaped when it was opened!

"Taken all round it was a brilliant day and Tim Webster deserves special mention for learning four songs so quickly and singing so well."

Those present-

First Tenor: Terry Stirzaker, Derek Parsons, Ron Williams.
Second Tenor: John Capell, Mike Fortune, Derek Lawrence
                      Francis Lewis, Brian Parkes, Tim Webster.
First Bass: Gordon Willetts, Martin Powe, Alf Anstee, Jack Dennis
                      John Blackmore, Alan Hooper, Terry Abbiss.
Second Bass: Jeff Garland, Duncan Hughes, Jim Leach.

Two of our number are pretty certain they contracted Covid-19 on that trip (they are both fine) and the organisors took the wise precaution of cancelling the events on subsequent days.

It was not long before we decided that meeting face to face was no longer an option. On March 16th, two days after our performances in Bath our next two engagements were cancelled due to the rapidly emerging crisis, one for The Red Cross and a visit to Four Lanes Choir in Cornwall.

The cancellation of the trip to Four Lanes was particularly sad because Gerald Toghill, a wonderfully bearded and moustached former mariner, who we inherited from Glastonbury Male Voice Choir had set his sights on returning to Redruth, his home territory, rather than submit to the rampant cancer that was in the process of overwhelming him. Gerald sadly passed away in July 2020 having managed to get home from the Hospice to celebrate his 83rd birthday. Due to the protracted lockdown we were able to send only a small choir contingent to sing at his funeral, but he will not be forgotten.

Our secretary Richard Salter expressed the situation very well in his note to the choir on March 16th:

"We had hoped that some men who wished to could continue to meet on Wednesday evenings, but for three reasons we no longer think this should happen.

(a) Today's stringent national advice urges people not to meet in groups- go to pubs, clubs, restaurants etc. This advice is for everyone, not just over-70s.
(b) We employ Hazel and Nick, and we must not make them feel they ought to

attend rehearsals as long as some men want to meet.

(c) Although we all enjoy meeting to sing, as long as we have no forthcoming concerts rehearsals as such we have no 'raison d'etre'.

"Adding those three factors together, if we were to continue to meet, and there were any adverse consequences arising from that, we would be held to have acted irresponsibly.

"Naturally we all hope that we shall be back in our familiar rows before too long but of course we cannot know today when that will be. Do look after yourselves and your families and those you care for. If you have particular difficulties which some choir member could help with, let us know. Meanwhile I'm sure many of us will 'meet' by phone, email and in our own ways as days and weeks go by."

Little did anyone know in March 2020 that we would still to this day (October 2021) be dealing with the dangers and complexities of the Covid-19 situation.

Our first job was to find a way to keep the choir together. Quite a few of the choir were not regular computer users, or even in some cases even owned a computer. We needed to find a way of creating a forum for people to continue to meet and, hopefully, sing together. On March 18th we had found the 'Zoom' system which was to become one of the mainstays of many choirs' continuity. It is quite likely we were one of the very first to use the video meeting facilities Zoom offers and after trawling the choir for their opinion held our first choir gathering online on March 25th after some one to one trials and an open house practice session in the morning before we took to the airwaves with our rehearsal.

Zoom proved to be no substitute for a 'proper' rehearsal but in the absence of any likelihood of physically meeting it did allow some degree of cohesion, and generated a lot of hilarity when 40 people tried to sing together over wildly different quality network connections - we soon realised that singing to ourselves was the only way with so many online at the same time. We rehearsed every Wednesday as normal and well over 50 members were engaged at least once with Zoom while over 40 were regulars. Throughout the spring and early summer we continued this process while trying to find a better set-up. We got used to the Zoom facilities and moved into break out rooms with leaders for different voices; Nick Thomas, Hazel Reed and John Pengelly were excellent leaders and this subdivision allowed many opportunities for group singing without it sounding ridiculous.

Musical Director Nick Thomas commented on our initiatives:

"It is impressive that we have so many attending the Zoom rehearsal when I hear that so many societies are struggling to keep it all going. The breakout rooms have been most useful and I am sure very beneficial. I have had feedback about this and it is very positive. I feel that the choir all realise the effort we are making to make this work successfully and are willing to run with this during these tricky times."

For a few weeks in the summer of 2020 we managed to arrange very limited face to face contact with massive precautions thanks to the Temple Methodist Church being prepared to work with us. Without Joanna Rossiter we would never have managed. But it was not to continue due to the increasing severity of the Covid-19 situation and it was not until September 2021 that we met as a complete choir for rehearsal once again.

We are all thankful that only a very few members have felt unable to return (and we completely understand) and a substantial choir started rehearsing for the 75th Anniversary Annual Concert due to be held at the Tacchi Morris Theatre on October 30th 2021. We were saddened that several choir members passed away during the 18 months we were unable to be together - Val Hill, Gerard Toghill, Malcolm Phillips, Dr John Crosby and Gilbert Fairs. Within the strictures of numbers in public spaces the choir managed to make strong representation at all these sad occasions.

8 WHAT WOULD WE DO WITHOUT OUR MUSICIANS

A choir is nothing without its singers. But it is everything if there is strong engagement with a professional music team. The Musical Director of the choir contributes so much to the quality, consistency, style and enjoyment for the choir itself, and also the audience.

Accompanists provide the essential discipline for every song. While the role of accompanist often requires being dropped in at the last moment the true professional can pick up the music and sound as if they have been playing it with the choir for ever. Rehearsals require an additional skill, patience... while the Musical Director or the choir (or both) consider and test different options for light and shade, timing and presentation.

There is one person who for nearly 50 years has influenced the choir, been loved by the choir and who valued the choir's friendship and all our music. Valerie Hill cut across the divide of conductor and accompanist and added something very special to the choir in doing so. She has her own section at the end of this chapter.

Up to 2006 there were a number of conductors and accompanists. The list brings us up to the recent period which is discussed in some detail.

	Conductor.	Accompanist.
1946.	Jeffrey Tottle.	Betty Morrison.
1949	Charles Oxland..	
1953	Freddie Goodliffe.	
1957	Stanley Jones.	
1960		Kathleen Woods.
1961		Miss. K. Greenwood.
1962	Ronald Tickner	
1963		Miss White.
1964.		Valerie Hill
1965	Douglas Shepherd.	
1974	Harold Culverwell.	Janet Bazley.
1975		No Accompanist.
1978	Chris. White	Mrs. V. Dyde, Miss Jo Andrews.
1982		Elisabeth Bell.
1992	R. Whitely,	
1993	Reg. Griffiths, F.E. Burroughes.	
1993	Reg. Griffiths, F.E. Burroughes.	
2000		Robert Murray.
2002		Valerie Hill (appointed Deputy Accompanist)
2003		Jason Baxter
2004		Hazel Reed, with Anne Parfit-Rogers assisting.
2004		Hazel Reed
2006	David Yates	Hazel Reed and Valerie Hill

Musical Director

Through the choir's 75 years there have been a number of Musical Directors of the highest quality and dedication. The choir would not be what it is today without them.

At the outset the person with the baton was called the Conductor. It was in 1951 during the tenure of Charles Oxland in the role that the title was changed to Musical Director, and it has remained so to the present day (although the terms are often used interchangeably) reflecting the wider involvement in choir management, music selection and involving recruitment of soloists, supporting groups and accompanists.

The first Conductor was **Jeffrey Tottle**, who had returned in July 1946 from his war-time service with the R.A.F. He was organist at St. Andrew's Church Rowbarton, and his accompanist was Betty Morrison. Both were well known in the town of Taunton. Jeffrey was a member of his family building firm, and a highly talented musician, having composed music from the age of 12. His works included organ pieces and all types of church music. Some of his choral pieces were dedicated to the Wessex Male Singers.

Jeffrey had a fine church choir at Rowbarton, and was known in the town as an excellent choir-trainer. His wife was Secretary of St. Andrew's Dramatic Society, and between them they organised many parish pantomimes and entertainments, Margaret writing the words and Jeff composing the music. He recruited several of his choir men at St. Andrews into the Wessex Male Singers, among them Cyril Salway. He died in 1991. We were pleased that Margaret was able to attend the Choir's Jubilee Concert.

He arranged and dedicate pieces to Betty Morrison and the choir, including Widdicombe Fair...

Charles Oxland, also well known in the Taunton area, succeeded Jeff in 1948. He had had a lifetime experience in training choirs and bands, and brought increased discipline and authority to the role. It was during his time in 1951 that the question arose of what the Conductor was to be called, and the term Musical Director was officially adopted. This is a very early use of this title for the Conductor, which has now become common with all sorts of musical groups and ensembles.

Charles Oxland was a Cornishman, and had conducted the Illogan Military

Band and the Cornish Miners' Male Voice Choir. He had also been Choirmaster at St. Andrew's Church during Jeffrey Tottle's war-time service. His style was distinctly formal, not of him would it ever be said as was said of his predecessor, "We are fortunate in having one who when off the rostrum is just 'Jeff' and one of us, without any of the eccentricities to which many musicians were addicted." He insisted on being called Mr. Oxland, and would not refer to choir members by their Christian name. He had by this time become organist at West Monkton Church.

Membership steadily increased, until it reached 34 members in 1952, although several 'were prevented from taking an active part in the choir.' (One wonders what the significance of their membership of the Choir was, if they did not actually sing with it. Or perhaps they only attended rehearsals and not concerts?). Oxland was greatly respected as a Conductor, though possibly he was less popular as a choir trainer than Tottle. Charles Oxland resigned in 1953 when he moved away from the area.

Freddie Goodliffe was appointed. The reason for his appointment is a slight mystery. He was for several years the Secretary of the Somerset Music Committee. He had no conducting experience, but apparently impressed the members, as the secretary P.G. Baker reported at the Annual General Meeting, with his customary bluntness, "It was agreed that we endeavour to secure the services of Mr. Goodliffe as our Conductor. Well, we have Mr. Goodliffe. You all know that he is very interested. This is his first effort as Conductor. He is improving and he must before going to Bristol. May I appeal to you all to give him support." At the time of his appointment the Choir recorded an average attendance at rehearsals of 23; the following year it had dropped to 17.

By 1956 membership was down to 15, and the Annual General Meeting rather belatedly noted a delay in starting rehearsals and a slackening of discipline. The Choir had (perhaps unadvisedly and unrealistically) auditioned with the B.B.C. West of England Region, and not surprisingly a rather sharp letter had come back stating that the choir was "not recommended for inclusion in the list of those available for broadcasting."

In style Goodliffe was much more informal and relaxed than his predecessor, so perhaps the members were tired of a martinet as Conductor. Goodliffe was not entirely oblivious to the decline in discipline and attendance. He hoped that attendance at rehearsals would be maintained so that the Choir could get down to the music for Bristol.He felt that local functions should take second place. Others in the Choir felt that local concerts were the Choir's staple diet.

Stan Jones was appointed to the vacant post of Musical Director after Freddie Goodliffe's resignation in 1957. Stan Jones was the Organist at Paul's Meeting House, (now Paul Street United Reformed Chapel) and also conductor of the Taunton Ladies' Choir. At his first A.G.M. he was able to report "Standards of singing had improved, although the standard of performance was not good." The following year he stated that the number of performances at concerts would be limited until there was an improvement in the standard of the Choir's work. He also commented that there would be no real improvement until the Choir took rehearsals seriously and not just as a night out with the boys.

In 1959 the Choir held the first of many combined concerts with the Taunton Ladies Choir. The Chairman noted that Mr. Jones "had shown the Choir the edge of his temper at times, which was no bad thing for the good of the Choir". Stan Jones retired in 1962 because of ill health. He continued as conductor of the Ladies' Choir for another year or two) and the Choir were fortunate through Sidney Holyoak, the County Music Advisor, to interest the late **Ron Tickner**, then Head of Music at Richard Huish Grammar School, and Organist and Choir-master at St. Mary Magdalene Parish Church to take over.

Ron Tickner

There is no doubt that Ron did not appreciate what he had let himself in for. He immediately cancelled most of the Choir's concerts, so that they only performed with the Taunton Ladies' Choir and at Wellington Blind School, in addition to the yearly visit to the massed Choirs concert at the Colston Hall Bristol.

The following year Ron had enough confidence in the Choir to increase the number of Concerts to three, and reported an improvement in the Choir, particularly in soft singing. However, the Choir still needed to watch the Conductor more, to get any real improvement.

In September 1963 **Miss Ruth White** succeeded Miss Greenwood who had moved to another teaching post, as accompanist, and **Miss Valerie Hill** in turn succeeded her in 1964. The choir now performed four concerts, and also attended the Taunton Music Festival, which it had not done since 1954.

By 1965 Ron felt that the state of his health meant he too must resign from leading the Choir, in order to concentrate on those areas he found more congenial. He was replaced by **Douglas Shepherd,**

Douglas Shepherd

Head of Music at Priorswood School, and, like Stan Jones, by this time also Conductor of the Taunton Ladies' Choir. The Choir gave three concerts, as well as attending the Taunton Festival and the Bristol Massed Choir Festival, and also gave a joint concert with the Taunton Ladies' Choir, which by now was establishing itself as an annual event.

In 1968 the Annual Concert was held with the Wellington Silver Band, which was to continue until 1995. In Shepherd's time the Choir increased in ability and confidence; at first he felt they should sing no more than four concerts a year, but this gradually increased each year, until by the end of his tenure of office in 1973, the Choir sang in seven concerts during the season.

1974 was a year of change again for the choir, with the appointment of **Harold Culverwell** as Conductor, and the retirement of Valerie Hill, who was replaced by **Janet Bazley,** another schoolteacher. She resigned the following year, although she offered to help out as needed, and so the Choir was without an accompanist for over two years, before the appointment of **Mrs. Veronica Dyde**, who only attended as required. Harold in the meantime filled a dual role as Conductor and Accompanist. Many of the Choir felt that this was unsatisfactory, and remarked that the Choir would be better off if it had a separate Accompanist.

Harold was a fine organist and choirmaster, in the Ron Tickner style, indeed possibly the better choir trainer. He had been Organist at Holy Trinity Church, Taunton since 1943, when he succeeded his teacher, Harry Lee, who had been organist at Holy Trinity from 1905. Harold had been a choirboy at Holy Trinity, and like David Gill, his parents and grandparents were regular worshippers at the church.

Harold was for many years the Deanery Choirmaster for the Diocesan Choral Festival, and in 1974, the year that he was appointed as Conductor of the Male Voice Choir, he was presented with the rare honour of a Fellowship of the Royal School of Church Music by Michael Ramsay, the Archbishop of Canterbury, for his services to Church Music in the town and diocese. It would have been interesting if he, like Ron, had stayed longer with the Choir. However, like Ron, he also retired ostensibly because of ill health in 1977, and **Mr. Chris. White**, later organist at St. Michael's Galmington, was appointed his successor. (Chris also followed Harold Culverwell as the Deanery Choirmaster for the Diocesan Choral Association, showing what a small village the musical world is.)

Chris White

Chris White's first hope was that the Choir would sing some music without copies, apparently unaware that almost every Conductor since 1946 had been expressing the same hope!

The following year he felt that the Choir were pushed to learn any more than the thirteen items that had been selected the last season. The following year he again hoped that the Choir would sing some pieces from memory, and the following year the need for a regular Accompanist was noted.

Chris. White remained as the Choir's conductor for 14 years and 142 Concerts. In his earlier years as Conductor he often had to remind members about their musical standards. In both 1977 and 1979 members felt that Concerts were too short, and that perhaps people were not getting their money's worth.

In 1988 the Choir complained that they sang too much religious music, but others felt that Male Voice Choirs traditionally sang a high proportion of hymns. The Conductor felt that the Choir would be pushed to learn more than

13 pieces to a suitable standard. But during his time the number of Concerts gradually increased to ten or eleven a year, though in his last year (1991-1992) he was still hoping that the Choir would aim to have about twelve items of music available to perform at any one time.

On the 27th of May 1992, the Choir said its official 'goodbye' to Chris with a buffet and presentation at the Victory Inn, at about the same time that Jeff Tottle, the first Conductor of the Choir died. Many members rightly felt that a definitive era of the Choir had come to an end.

Chris White recalls his time with the choir as a thoroughly enjoyable period. "I always felt extremely well supported with a strong sense of fellowship through-out the choir and with myself. I hope that during that time things were not taken too seriously while giving performances to the best of our ability.

"The choir always suffered from a shortage of first tenors during Chris White's tenure and a surfeit of first basses. Consequently it was quite difficult if there were absences for concerts. At one concert in Huish Episcopi church we reached the halfway point when a solo was scheduled. I looked at the choir and realised that the soloist wasn't there! There was nothing for it, other than I had to do it myself. I think it went unnoticed."

R. Whitely had the unenviable task of following Chris White and he found great difficulties in coming to terms with a Choir which was still run as much as a social institution as a serious performing group.

His experience with choral music was as a bass soloist and assistant conductor of Bradford Police Male Voice Choir. Now retired, he lived at Middlezoy, and was organist at Fivehead Church, His expectations of the Choir were rather different from what they were themselves used to. His time as Conductor was not a happy one either for himself or the Choir. It was with a sense of relief for both parties that they decided to part company in March 1993, and for the remaining two months of the season the choir was led by Reg Griffiths until their new Conductor could take over.

During this difficult period, when the Choir had lost many members, the Committee wisely decided to act with caution in appointing a replacement, and after advertising the post, (for the first time ever) two external candidates, and Reg Griffiths from the Choir put their names forward.

Each candidate was invited to take the Choir for a rehearsal, the members voting for their preferred option. As a result, **Dr. F. E. Burroughes** was selected, although the Choir were perhaps disarmed by his initial charm and ease of manner. They were soon to have a sharp awakening! They may have also felt sorry that on his way to the test rehearsal, a stone flung up by a passing car where the Corporation was resurfacing East Reach shattered his windscreen, making it one of the most expensive auditions he attended.

Dr. F.E.Buroughes

After study at Southampton and Oxford Universities, Dr. Burroughes taught for several years as Head of Music in schools in the Cotswolds and Midlands, before returning to his home town of Yeovil.

His first interest lay with choral music, although he was a highly experienced orchestral conductor. As well as the Male Voice Choir he conducted several other Choral Societies, Chamber Choirs, and Operatic Societies in the county and beyond. He was later organist at St. John's Church in Taunton, and also at Lufton, near Yeovil, where he built and gave an organ in memory of his parents. He was also the South West Area Chairman for the Association of British Choral Directors, (a body dedicated to raising professional standards among conductors) serving on its National Council.

The new Conductor's first priority was recruiting. The membership had fallen to twenty-seven nominal members, but this included several who were no longer singing regularly with the Choir; for example one member had retired to Spain and lived there for six months of the year, while another had not sung with the choir, because of his wife's poor state of health, for four or five years. Altogether, the Choir had fallen to just about twenty singing members, which given the low turnout of members who actually sang at Concerts, was a dangerously small number to keep the Choir viable.

With hard work and endless publicity, recruiting displays in Taunton Library, interviews on B.B.C. Somerset Sound and word of mouth, the membership increased to 47 within a couple of years.

The next problem to be faced was the actual quality of the Choir's performances. Not only musically, but also in presentation, the Choir, (although it did not then know it) was ready for change, and had at last adopted a smart uniform rather than the previous 'ad hoc' mixture of dark suits and dinner jackets. The Uniform was agreed in early 1994, some 43 years after the idea was first raised. Many members over the years having been involved in the seemingly unending saga, but it fell to Brian Reynolds to achieve the honour of finally resolving the whole question. Many complimentary comments were made about the uniform when it was worn for the first time.

The vastly improved stage appearance led to an improvement in
sound as well, and it was aided by the realisation that the Choir was soon to celebrate it's Golden Jubilee. The Silver Jubilee in 1972 had passed by default, the Committee felt that it was 'unnecessary to mark it in any kind of way', although there had been a Silver Jubilee
dinner, which the Chairman regretted 'had not come up to the standard he had hoped for.'

The Conductor seized the opportunity of the Golden Jubilee to effect some radical changes in the way the Choir functioned. A small Jubilee Committee, consisting of John Blackmore the Concert Secretary, Brian Reynolds the Treasurer, the Secretary Geoff Ede, and the Conductor, planned a whole year of events, which would celebrate the Choir's new lease of life.

The first hurdle to be overcome was the Annual Concert. Since 1968 this had become a shared event with Wellington Silver Band, and was held in St. Andrew's Church Rowbarton, the proceeds going to Abbeyfields. The Conductor was adamant that the Jubilee Annual Concert would be given by the Choir alone, would be held in a prestigious venue, and the Choir would retain the proceeds. After many acrimonious Committee meetings the Conductor had his way, and the Brewhouse Theatre was booked for the first Saturday in June 1996. The Brewhouse had been built in 1977, after many years of effort by a dedicated band of Tauntonians who were determined to create a Centre for the Arts in the town.

This was the first time that the Choir had sung in the Theatre, nineteen years after it had opened, and sixteen years after the Wellington Band had given their first concert there. Sheelagh Lee- Ewers, host of a magazine programme on B.B.C. Somerset Sound was invited to be compere for the occasion, and the soloist was Terri Ladd, accompanied by Chris Ball. The concert was duly held and sold out. All the surviving conductors of the Choir attended, and the Choir was particularly pleased to welcome Jeff Tottle's widow.

The Golden Jubilee Season

During the Jubilee season, the Choir had travelled over a far wider area than ever before, giving concerts in Devon and Dorset, as well as all over Somerset. The Jubilee season ended with the Choir presenting a Massed Gala of Male Voice Choirs in St. George's Hall, Exeter, the only venue locally big enough to hold such an event.

But behind the scenes there were other fundamental changes happening as well. The Choir started to overhaul its Library, immediately removing all illegal photocopies, and increasing the number in each set to 60. The first year £866 was spent on this, and a further two thousand pounds over the next three years.

The Choir extended the end of its season from mid May, to the middle of June. The new Conductor initiated a series of Workshops and Singing Classes which were held for six or seven weeks after the end of the season, effectively leaving only the month of August as a close season. In addition, occasional singing and sight-reading days with visiting tutors, such as Penny and Neil Jenkin from Brighton, were held, as well as encouraging individual participation in vocal classes of local music festivals.

The Choir was encouraged to expand its horizons by taking part in various Choir Competitions, including Sainsbury's Choir of the Year, the Jersey International Choir Festival, other more local Music Festivals, and Combined Galas in Manchester and London Royal Albert Hall. The Choir began to include music from the Renaissance and Baroque periods in its library, and also commissioned and had composed for it new music, including several pieces arranged or composed by its Conductor. The number of concerts presented each season increased to fifteen or sixteen, and for the first time in 1997 over £2000 was raised for various good causes by the Choir's efforts. The figure had increased to over £3500 annually by 2003.

In 2005 Dr Burroughes reflected on his time with the choir in advance of the 2006 Diamond Jubilee. One alteration he hoped to be considered was that it should be unusual for members to miss a concert. The season just finished showed that other than the Annual Concert there were never more than 80% of the choir present. He felt that in any other type of musical activity this would be totally unacceptable.

He did not want Taunton Deane to be like all other Male Voice Choirs. While it is interesting to see what other choirs do, if only to ensure we do not make the same mistake he felt that we should try to have more imagination and be more 'musical' than most other choirs. He was sure that to secure any future for the Choir we must insist on the highest standards musically, in our presentation and in our organisation.

After 14 years with the Choir, F.E. Burroughes gave notice of his intention to resign at the end of the Diamond Jubilee season.

Our retiring conductor bids the choir farewell

"I was unable to see absolutely everyone after the Concert, but I would just like to say how well I thought you sang, even those of you who are still using copies, and how much the audience obviously enjoyed it. Thank you too for my gifts. I shall use the interesting piece of paper to buy a couple of trees for my garden; a Gingko Biloba, and a Gordonia Altahama.

"They are both extremely long-lived species; we shall see whether they outlast the Taunton Deane Male Voice Choir. I hope your Chairman read out my good wishes and thanks to you all at the A.GM. However, life goes on. After the Jubilee concert, I hastened to Paris for a few days complete break. While I was there, I managed to get to quite a few concerts and recitals, including two male voice choir concerts. It was a fascinating trip and I am pleased to hear that the editor intends to include a more detailed account in the next edition of Voice-Male.

"I finished off a series of rehearsals with Axminster Choral Society by the beginning of July and am now gloriously free of all rehearsals until the beginning of September. However, that does not mean I am not doing any music at all; I am busy at the moment marking up orchestral parts for St.Mary's Orchestra next term and trying to get the score of *The Kingdom* into my head for The Choral Society.

"As I write this, I have just finished packing for another week in Paris for a meeting with a group of German and Belgian organists and organ builders. We are celebrating the success recently achieved by Europe-wide enthusiasts in altering a piece of misguided European legislation which would have prevented organ builders from repairing lead pipe-work in organs because they were classified as 'electronic instruments' of all things.

"The end of August is the Annual Conference of the Association of British Choral Directors in Gateshead. I hope to go if I am feeling well enough, but it is a long trek. September sees the start of the new term, and at the beginning of October I shall be in Birmingham for a
Gala Concert celebrating an Elgar Centenary. Later in the month, I shall be in Jersey for the International Choir Festival, and I have just accepted a booking to lecture to the British Institute of Organ Studies next February. I have concerts lined up until February 2008.

"Apart from that, I am enjoying my retirement! I shall continue to be interested in your future progress as a Choir, and I look forward to coming to hear you again under your new Conductor.

"My best wishes to you all. I hope you continue to enjoy your musical and social life together."
Francis Burroughes.

Having been given ample warning of Dr. Burroughes retirement, the Choir took the opportunity to assess its philosophy, and under the energetic leadership of the Chairman, Tony Slavin, produced a Policy for the Choir which expressed the Choir's aspirations, and its objectives for the medium and the long term. This was used as a basis to determine the sort of Musical Director they were looking for. The post was advertised, but applications were slow in coming, and the Committee had to begin to consider the probability of at last having to increase the honoraria offered to its professional musicians, to attract the calibre of expertise which the Choir desired and deserved.

The problem of finding a replacement for Francis Burroughes was eventually solved in dramatic fashion when **David Yates**, a second tenor in the choir, emerged from the ranks and astonished the rest of the choir by admitting that he had appropriate skills as organist and pianist and already conducted another choir in Bridgwater. As a side issue, when his musical interests permitted, he had previously been a rocket scientist and university lecturer! David took over at the start of the 2006/2007 season and proved to be both competent and popular, a combination not always present in some former conductors.

David Yates

David was our Musical Director from 2006 to 2013. He recalls his time with the choir:

"Although born in Blackpool, I spent nearly all my school years in Taunton. My love of choral music began when I was a choirboy at Taunton St James's, which had a good choir in those days, followed by the chapel choir at my senior school. Professionally I am an engineer, having worked in the aerospace and nuclear power industries, then lectured in three universities. However in my spare time I was a church organist and choirmaster, and an accompanist or musical director in amateur show societies.

"I returned to Taunton on my retirement, and looked around for social activities. I joined a number of choirs, including TDMVC. However, I had only been a member for two years when the then Musical Director, Francis Burroughes, retired. Finding a replacement was proving difficult, so I offered to fill in until one was found. After I had been thoroughly checked over by the chairman, my offer was accepted, and I did the job for seven years.

"My new job was made easy by the friendliness, enthusiasm and team spirit of the members. I think you can tell a lot about the health of a choir by the time people arrive for a rehearsal. I have known some where you think you have come on the wrong night if you arrive five minutes early. Not so TDMVC. Fifteen minutes before time the rehearsal room is already buzzing.

"I look back on my term of office as seven wonderfully enjoyable years: hard work, but a great privilege to be given such a responsibility. The highlights, the times which I remember best, were the trips away to sing with other choirs, particularly the Cornwall Festival, of which we attended three during that time. Such activities are immensely valuable in bonding the choir together, and giving an extra incentive to work on and improve our performances. It also enabled us to see, hear and learn from a wide variety of other choirs, including a number from overseas (I particularly remember the Estonians and the group from Brittany), and youth choirs (Czech, Manchester Boys). For me the festivals were also a great opportunity to hear the competition choirs in performance.

"After all these years I can still remember nearly all the jokes told at a five-choir concert by the compere, introduced as a local farmer, (was it Bruce Taylor himself?) – the camels in Newquay Zoo, the doctor's waiting room, and "Our sponsors, NatWest Bank, have sent their choir along tonight, and they will sing "For you alone". We also visited some beautiful places at a time of year when Cornwall is probably at its best! I hope I will be able to go along next time there is a "Cornwall". In years when there was no festival to visit we went to Bournemouth, St Austell Brewery and Basingstoke, again memorable occasions where we met local choirs.

"When I joined TDMVC, my wife, who was still working and living in Staffordshire at the time, was a little surprised. Now, directly or indirectly, we owe most of our friends in Taunton to my membership of the choir. I still direct a church choir and play the organ at Pitminster, a job which I was recruited for by a TDMVC member. I also sing with a couple of other choral societies, and occasionally in the chorus of Somerset Opera.

Nick Thomas

Nick studied music and eduction at the College of St Mark and St John's (Marjons), Plymouth and spent much of his working life in schools as Head of Music, first in Cranleigh, Surrey and latterly at Kingsmead, Wiveliscombe.

Up until December 2011 Nick was Musical Director of the West Somerset singers. He has been Musical Director at St George's Church Wilton, Flute Teacher at Kings College Taunton and a vocal coach for many very talented local musicians.

He has directed many stage musicals and has performed with a number of operatic societies. He teaches woodwind, piano, brass and singing in and around Taunton and also pays flute and accordion in local folk group Tranters Folly

Nick recalls his first encounter with the choir. "I first conducted the choir at an out of season concert on the 29th June 2013 at St Mary Magdalene church in Taunton and a week later a concert in Barnstaple Devon because David Yates was unavailable. I expressed an interest in taking on the role as Musical Director and was interviewed on 30th July 2013.

"I took up the baton with the choir on 11th September 2013 and have been there ever since. I am eternally grateful for the help and guidance I received from the late Valerie Hill, who kept an eagle eye on my work and progress each week, and on the bass section during rehearsals. Our accompanist Hazel Reed has been a positive and respected member of the musical team who has been great to work with.

"I am very grateful for the support of the 3 Chairmen I have worked with over the years, Tony Slavin, John Capell and Paull Robathan and also our very supportive President David Gill"

Nick has often taken the choir out of their comfort zone, but with faith and increasing confidence has led the choir to perform many difficult and challenging songs. Adding his own skills on the flute (memorably on *Tell My Father*) and accordion Nick has added a new dimension to much of our repertoire.

The choir has often been a platform for young up and coming musicians, introduced to the choir by Nick. Together with a roster of interesting and varied guest performers at concerts the choir under Nick's baton has gone from strength to strength.

Our 75th year Annual Concert will see Cameron Rolls perform some of the great Tenor works including *Nessun Dorma*.

Elaine Thomas, Nick's wife, is closely associated with the choir and has accompanied the choir in many rehearsals. On the retirement of Hazel Reed as our long standing accompanist Elaine agreed to assist Nick with rehearsals conducting and accompanying, and is proving to be a critical and constructive member of the music team.

Elaine has been the Music Director at Wilton Church and until recently has been the Music Director for The New Horizons. The choir now has to cope with two experienced MDs, and seem to be enjoying the double act at rehearsals.

Nick and Elaine's roles were reversed with New Horizons Ladies Choir.

New Horizons has been a welcome part of the music scene in Taunton, and several of the members at any time have been partners with members of Taunton Deane Male Voice Choir. The two choirs have sung together at the Albert Hall, at jointly arranged Christmas concerts, at the bandstand in Vivary Park for Christmas Carols and on a number of other occasions.

Assistant Musical Director

Chris Grabham

Chris joined the choir in January 2016, whilst completing his A-Levels at Richard Huish College. His first concert with the choir occurred in April 2016 at St. Mary's Church, Bridgwater. Upon graduating from college in the summer, Chris began to take his musical work more seriously, with a view to becoming a professional conductor and/or composer one day.

In May 2017, he was appointed as the Wiveliscombe Town Band's Director of Music and shortly afterwards also began conducting professional productions of musical theatre, most notably at the Brewhouse Theatre. Shortly after his introduction to the professional world of music, Chris began to study for a diploma in Film Scoring & Music Production, two fields which really interest him. Following successful interviews and auditions, Chris was later offered a place to study for a Bachelor of Music degree in Composition for Film & Theatre; after 5 years of Conservatoire-based training, his course is due to finish in June 2022.

Chris has aspirations to become a famous Conductor and/or Composer, working within the specialist fields of Film/TV & Theatre.

The choir remembers Chris' leadership on *Roman War Song* at Launceston that brought the house down in front of many seasoned choral experts.

Accompanist

Betty Morrison

Betty Morrison was the choir's first accompanist and lived in the parish of St. Andrew's Rowbarton, in Station Road. She had a daughter Sonia, who played the cello. At one of the Choir's concerts in the Corfield Hall, (now Orange Tree Interiors) in April 1958, in aid of the restoration appeal for St. Mary's Church, Sonia was the soloist for the choir. Betty was not only the Choir accompanist but was very often the organiser of the Choir's social events. It was therefore with considerable regret that the Choir received news of her resignation in March 1960, because of ill-health. She died about a year later in 1961.

Hazel Read

"My first attempts at mastery of a keyboard were probably when I was aged about four, when I remember sitting with my grandfather at the harmonium almost certainly playing something nonsensical on the keys while he somehow operated the pedals. I presume that is what inspired my parents to let me begin piano lessons when I was just five, steadily working my way through the graded examinations of the Associated Board of the Royal Schools of Music until I was seventeen. During these years singing and recorder lessons and exams were added, and home tuition in brass, my father being an accomplished euphonium player. The awful screech that came from my cousin's violin when I first tried it put me off playing strings for life, though a guitar became the 'in thing' in the 60's.

"There are just two regrets about that era. My headmistress would not even allow me to audition for extra Saturday morning lessons at nearby Trinity College, London as it would apparently have interfered with my general edu-cation! Later, although under a different Head, the sixth form curriculum did not cater for a friend and I to take A-level music although we would at the time have had very little extra work to do for it. I will never know whether I could have succeeded in either of those areas. Thankfully though, our wonderfully encouraging music mistress gave up some of her free time to guide us through sufficient set works for the O-level exam, the certificate at least proving that we had studied music alongside the 'normal' subjects!

"Soon after leaving school I was able to take an extra-mural diploma exam at the London College of Music. The Principal at that time was Dr William Lloyd Webber, father of the now famous sons. It was somewhat nerve-wracking to find that he was my Examiner. He was kind, but when he chuckled after I had taken my sight-reading test I remember just looking at him, wondering what on earth I had done to cause such a reaction. He then said "You are an accompanist aren't you. You kept the timing going well but there were a few notes missing". His comment on the results paper was 'Keep up the accompanying'. Did he have fifty years in mind, playing regularly at church and working with a fair few choirs and soloists?

"In 1986 I was married and moved to Somerset. I soon found myself playing the piano at church again, and a new friend invited me to join the local choral society. This opened up a whole new range of music for me which I thoroughly enjoyed, and I was actually able to *sing* and not play! A dozen ladies from the main choir hurriedly became a chamber choir in a stop-gap situation, but as often happens the temporary nature of that group lasted for about six years, so I again found myself accompanying when we weren't singing madrigals.....!

"It was also great to be able to join an adult recorder group and a handbell team during that time, and to use my experience to run music groups at the day centre where I worked. Music therapy was just emerging when I left school but involved degree standard education. This time I chose not to try for that, but the opportunity to help disabled people to enjoy all kinds of music, even unofficially, rather made up for it!

"After some sixteen years based in Chard we moved to Hemyock, just over into Devon, in 2001. It eventually proved impossible to work, be the Pastor's wife, support my elderly parents in Poole and keep up with my usual music activities. The village singers and handbell team filled the gap until I saw an advertisement for an accompanist for TDMVC in the local newspaper. I had left my work in Chard and my parents were now living locally so I applied. At least that would give me something to practice for! I knew the then Musical Director, Dr Francis Burroughes, to be rather a perfectionist, but he took me on, along with Anne Parfitt-Rogers, and we all worked together very happily for a year until she left for university. I am still here over sixteen years later, having also worked with David Yates, and now with Nick Thomas.

"Different Musical Director's preferences have meant many different styles of song and some challenges, but it has certainly involved practice! In the 2005 annual concert Anne and I subtly played part of a difficult accompaniment as a duet, but later came *The Battle Hymn of the Republic*, Mayotte's *Lord's Prayer*, *Speed your Journey* and *Bohemian Rhapsody* which all had to be played solo, and as for people who write in five or six sharps – no comment! *Rhythm of Life* was also a lot more enjoyable when Chris Grabham and I had the chance to play the accompaniment written as a duet as just that.

"I have unexpectedly found myself at the front a few times, most notably at a very breezy and cold Menin Gate, but I am very much a team player, and so prefer to be in the background supporting the team. The CD recordings, Cornwall festivals, overseas visits, cathedrals, parish churches, village halls and the open air – all have made special memories, along with the joys (and occasionally problems) of presenting live music.

"Val Hill, as a former accompanist and conductor over many years, was my mentor and was literally my 'right-hand man' as a most notable page-turner when things were going at any pace. She had been there herself and knew exactly when to flip the page without any indication from me! I owe a lot to her patience and experience and miss her very much as both colleague and friend.

"I am not quite certain how I came upon the position, but for some time have been acting as the choir welfare officer, so rather back to my professional roots in the old County Welfare Department! It is quite difficult to keep an eye on such a large group of people when I am sitting with my back to most at rehearsal. I have known some of the men for many years and soon notice if they are missing but often need to rely on others to keep me informed about newer members. As much concern and support is shown for each other as for the charities for whom we raise funds and has been commended by members and friends alike.

"In some circles I would not be regarded as a true accompanist as I cannot transpose 'live' very reliably or play much by ear, and I have never been the most technically able pianist, but I am so glad that I was given the opportunity to be a part of the team that is TDMVC and to put to use what Dr Lloyd Webber recognized in me.

"Sadly I have felt it necessary to retire from playing at concerts but will continue to do what I can, as long as I can keep up with the conductor and my now rather over-used fingers allow me to play........ without too many notes missing!"

Valerie Hill

Valerie (Val) Hill took over from Ruth White as accompanist in 1964. She retired in 1974. She rejoined the choir in 2002 as assistant accompanist. She left the choir through ill health in 2017 and died in July 2019.

Val grew up in Exeter. After teacher training her studies continued at the Royal Academy of Music. Soon after arriving in Taunton to teach at Weirfield School in 1964 she joined Taunton Deane Male Voice Choir as accompanist. She served for 10 years, mostly with Doug Shepherd as conductor. On leaving she was proud to be made an Honorary Life Member and remained the only lady member for many years.

As Head of Music at Weirfield she particularly enjoyed directing the music for their major stage productions, including *Oklahoma*, *The King and I*, *Fiddler on the Roof* and *The Sound of Music*.

After a year as Director of Music at Taunton Preparatory School when Weirfield moved to Taunton School Valerie finished full-time teaching and became accompanist to the Reg Griffiths Singers when Barbara Gimlett retired. Soon afterwards she was invited to rejoin the main choir and assisted with accompanying and conducting.

Her memory is strong in the minds of so many choir members through the years, and it is hard to put into words the mutual affection that existed between the choir and Val. Perhaps her own words she left for her own funeral that took place at Rowbarton Methodist Church on 9th August say it best.

"It has been a privilege to work with the TDMVC. They have been so supportive and helpful and have taken little apparent notice of my physical problems. They have also put up with me bossing them around.

"It would be lovely if the Taunton Deane Male Voice Choir would sing. I have valued their friendship and ALL their music. I would most like to have *Gwahoddiad* - perhaps plus something they think appropriate."

The choir turned up in numbers and sang *Gwahoddiad* and *What would I do without my Music.*

Val's cousin Winnie Bryant wrote us the day after the funeral saying how pleased and grateful everyone was that the choir took part. Everyone was delighted and "Valerie would have been thrilled to know they were doing this for her."

Winnie went on to say "I think we all learnt more about Valerie yesterday, and the huge part music played in her life. We know that she treasured her time with the choir and would like to thank them all not only for yesterday but also for the many years they worked with her and their kindness to her."

Jack Dennis, whose original material has been fundamental to this book wrote about Val after we heard the sad news of her death.

"Val was in charge of music at the independent Weirfield School in Taunton for many years and inspired many generations of pupils to enjoy and pursue their interest in music. She produced and arranged numerous concerts and recitals during her time at the school. Val was a highly talented pianist and musician and passed on her enthusiasm to her pupils. Sadly a stroke curtailed her playing career.

"She originally joined the choir as accompanist in 1964 coming to the rescue after a period of having three accompanists in four years. She remained in post until 1974 having done an excellent job.

"In 2001 a chance meeting with the late choir legend Alan Richards persuaded Val to return to the choir after an absence of 27 years. She eventually took on the post of Assistant Musical Director and held this position until 2017 when increasing ill health finally forced her into retirement.

"During her early years in post she mainly assisted the accompanist by turning the pages of music. However, she eventually did more teaching and conducting. Val had an amazing ability to pick out wrong notes and mistakes and whenever she walked around the rehearsal room or behind the choir panic immediately ensued!

"She instituted a 'note-bashing' session on Monday evenings which members found invaluable, and it was posssible on occasion to hold split rehearsals, working the tenors and basses separately. This cut down the learning time for new music and consequently gradually led to an expansion of the repertoire.

"Val was always kind, encouraging and patient and sought to be as positive as possible when teaching or introducing new songs. The choir always seemed to make a special effort when she conducted, particularly at Annual Concerts. Her clear and precise conducting style was always much appreciated.

"She always gave generously of her free time when helping us prepare for our various Royal Albert Hall performances.

"Val made a very special contribution to the choir and is very much missed by us all."

9 TAUNTON AND TAUNTON DEANE

Taunton's civic and mayoral history

75 years ago residents of the town of Taunton were governed by Taunton Borough Council. Sadly the town's history had been marked by dramatic periods of instability. The content of this chapter has been provided by Adrian Prior-Sankey MBE, Mayor of Taunton Deane 2002-2003.

Since 2009 the Mayor of Taunton Deane has been the patron of our choir. In 2019 the status of the authority changed and a Mayor of Taunton was elected, who then honoured us by being our patron. At the same time as the 2019 change of status the Chair of Somerset West and Taunton also became our patron recreating and further extending the wider patronage afforded by the previous mayors of Taunton Deane.

A chequered reputation

The town had enjoyed a chequered reputation regarding its loyalty (or lack of it) to successive monarchs. In the 15th century it saw a skirmish during the Wars of the Roses and hosted the second Cornish uprising of Perkin Warbeck and his 6,000-strong army which surrendered to Henry VII in Taunton Castle. During the early years of the English Civil War Taunton changed hands several times but latterly declared for parliament and the Castle was besieged for 12 months. It was defended by Robert Blake, with the consequential destruction of many medieval and Tudor buildings. In 1685 James, Duke of Monmouth, an illegitimate son of Charles II, having led a rebellion rallying support across the

West Country, proclaimed himself King in Taunton's High Street prior to his subsequent defeat at the Battle of Sedgemoor. The ensuing Bloody Assizes held in Taunton Castle were presided over by Judge Jeffreys who pronounced the death sentence on nearly 200 rebels found guilty of treason.

Borough status

Given the vicissitudes of the town it is hardly surprising to learn that Taunton did not obtain a charter of incorporation as a Borough until 1627. It was renewed in 1677, but lapsed in 1792 owing to vacancies for the members of the corporate body. Taunton was not reincorporated until 1877. With the designation as a Borough councillors were entitled to elect one of their number to chair its meetings and be accorded the dignity and privileges of a Mayor, commonly acknowledged to be the first citizen.

Mayors in the Victorian era and the early 20th century were usually those who had distinguished themselves in commerce before or whilst holding civic office.

Many mayors were generous benefactors, gifting regalia and silverware to the benefit (and sometimes embarrassment) of their heirs and successors.

The Court Leet

Prior to the granting of a charter, towns such as Taunton were largely administered by a Lord of the Manor and members of a Court Leet, precursor of modern trading standards and public health provision. Taunton's manorial and Court Leet heritage is today preserved only in a ceremonial and honorific form by elder brethren representative of retired public servants or past civic and business leaders.

The Coat of Arms

Until 1937 the town used a coat of arms featuring the imperial crown and a rather depressed looking cherub. When the College of Arms became aware they reflected on the town's ambivalence to the monarchy and dictated that the

Saxon crown of King Ina should be used below a more cheerful cherub. The 'illegal' crests are still displayed on significant structures around the town such as Vivary Park gates and the town bridge.

Taunton Deane Borough Council 1975 – 2019

April Fools' Day 1974 was the date appointed by the Local Government Act of 1972 for the merger of the Municipal Borough of Taunton with the local authorities hitherto responsible for the rural hinterland and the neighbouring town of Wellington. The newly created authority was initially named 'Taunton Deane District Council' but, following concern for the apparent loss of dignity for the County Town, a plea was made to parliament for the bestowing of Borough status and in 1975 the council settled into its 44 year operation. Taunton Deane Borough Council elected one of its members to serve as Mayor, chairing full meetings of the council. With one exception each of the Mayors of Taunton Deane served only once for one year. As what is termed a 'principal authority' with borough status, Taunton Deane's Mayor took precedence at gatherings of Mayors in the County who were variously chairpersons of charter trustees, parishes or town Councils.

Somerset West and Taunton Council 2019 onwards

By 2019 external pressure from the government of the day to address a financial problem facing the neighbouring West Somerset District Council led to a merger with Taunton Deane Borough Council. To the surprise of many, the larger number of Taunton-focused councillors welcomed the new name of the successor body which gave precedence to the rural element and 'Somerset West and Taunton Council' held its first meeting in May. On this occasion forethought had been given to the consequent loss of the mayoralty.

The legislation to establish the new authority included provision for the councillors representing the 'unparished' area of Taunton to meet as Charter Trustees and to appoint from among their number one who would take on the title and ceremonial role of Mayor of Taunton. It is thought that following a period of consultation (and possible creation of one or more parish councils from within the area affected), the Charter Trustees will evolve into a Town Council of which the chairperson will be styled as the Mayor of Taunton.

The roles of the present day Mayor and Chair

At the time of its formation in 2019 Somerset West and Taunton Council published clarification of the differing roles of Mayor and Chair:

The Mayor of Taunton represents the unparished area of Taunton - specifically they represent 'the town, the community and local democracy'.

The Mayor can use their office to raise money for specific charities, celebrate success in the town, 'be the face of the town in times of sadness' and welcome visitors.

The Chair of Somerset West and Taunton Council has five main duties: Promote District wide initiatives, host high profile visitors, attend events of regional, national or international significance, attend events aimed at enhancing the District's economic and social situation, wellbeing of the community, and being the conscience of the Council.

Future local government changes

In the background of the most recent local government changes is the push by rival politicians to shake up the whole structure to create a unitary council responsible for all local authority services. This will mean the merger of the present district and county councils to create one Unitary Authority to govern the population currently served by Somerset County Council.

This should not affect the aspiration to create (or should that be re-create?) a town council for Taunton chaired by one very privileged citizen who, for a short period, may enjoy the title and dignity as Mayor of Taunton.

Our patrons since 2009-10 have been

Mayor of Taunton Deane

- · 2009-2010 Bob Bowrah
- · 2010-2011 Jefferson Horsley
- · 2011-2012 Steve Brooks
- · 2012-2013 Terry Hall
- · 2013-2014 Libby Lisgo
- · 2014-2015 Dave Durdan
- · 2015-2016 Marcia Hill
- · 2016-2017 Vivienne Stock-Williams
- · 2017-2018 Hazel Prior-Sankey
- · 2018-2019 Catherine Herbert

Mayor of Taunton

- · 2019-2021 Francesca Smith
- . 2021-   Susan Lees

Chair of Somerset West and Taunton Council

- · 2019-   Hazel Prior-Sankey

A number of past mayors have commented on their association with the choir.

Cllr. Vivienne Stock-Williams patron 2016-2017

"It was a joy to attend concerts given by Taunton Deane Male Voice Choir during my year as Patron of the choir and Taunton Deane Borough Mayor (2016-17). The popular repertoire selected and joie-de-vie of the singers, combined with their consummate skill, ensured that the concert venue was always packed – many of the audience being regular attendees.

"Representatives from my three chosen Mayoral charities – Children's Hospice South West, National Garden Scheme Apprentice Scheme and Reminiscence Learning – were delighted to be invited to attend TDMVC's performance at their annual fund-raising Mayoral Charity Concert and were impressed by both the public spiritedness and dedication of the performers.

"Congratulations to the choir on achieving their 75th anniversary and I wish them continued camaraderie and success long into the future."

Councillor Catherine Herbert, patron 2018-2019

"As Mayor there are many things you discover that you have connections to. The TDMVC was one such obligation, the Mayor is patron I was told, 'So what does a patron do I asked?' Well you go to the concerts was pretty much the sum of it, so it seemed. I duly attended the first concert I was invited to at the Tacchi Morris, was sat with the choir's President, David Gill, with whom I was familiar , so we chatted away!

"The concert started and I was taken on a journey of emotion, of hearing the marvellous sounds and seeing how much the choir enjoyed performing together. Afterwards I was invited to join them in the bar for a drink and what is known as the "after glow". They just can't stop singing! Over a few drinks the songs flowed and the true joy of joining together in song was obvious.

"I was privileged to be allowed to attend a couple of rehearsals, being a patron was something I took very seriously! To hear the choir practice, build their knowledge of a song and then hear it performed all together was really great.

"It was especially moving to me as a military wife as they were holding a special anniversary concert to mark 100 years since the end of the Great War and the pieces were very moving.

"For my own concert I was thrilled that knowing my enthusiasm for show tunes the choir had some of these included so I could sing along!

"Music is such a gift, it can make you smile, it can bring you to tears (I am not sure how many times they sang *Tell my Father* but it gets me every time). Taunton Deane Male Voice Choir is a marvel, to witness the unity and joy was an honour and being patron was truly the icing on my Mayoral year's cake!"

Councillor Francesca Smith, patron 2019-2020

"As the Mayor of Taunton I was so pleased to be Patron of the Taunton Deane Male Voice Choir. Attending various concerts and listening to all types of music so beautifully sung was a lovely experience.

"I especially enjoyed attending the rehearsal session at the Temple Methodist Church, and listening to all the hard work that goes into practising the repertoire. Being Mayor during the COVID lockdown I was also pleased to attend the virtual cheque presentation and listen again to another rehearsal session. I love the camaraderie between the members of the choir but also the professionalism of the performances.

"Thank you for making me most welcome to your concerts and rehearsals and also for raising so much money towards the Mayor's charity."

Councillor Bob Bowrah was the first patron of the Choir 2009-2010. To commemorate the first concert where the Mayor was our patron a certificate was issued to the choir. We treasure the relationship as it continues into the future.

10 OFFICERS AND COMMITTEE MEMBERS

The choir would not be what it is today without massive commitment from Chairmen and Committee Members over many years.

We would like to pay tribute to the Officers and Committee Members who, over the years, have put in hundreds of hours of work to keep the choir functioning.

Cyril Salway was appointed to the vital task of Choir Secretary at the first meeting. In those days the Secretary was virtually the sole executive officer and dealt with all the normal day-to-day details of choir organisation, as well as acting as concert promoter and organising venues and soloists.

Cyril remained a stalwart member of the choir for many years after his retirement as secretary in 1951, eventually singing with the choir at their Golden Jubilee concert in 1996, the only founder member still to be active in the choir at that time.

In 1952 R. J. Lewis was appointed Chairman, and his son, who had a year or two earlier joined the choir on leaving the Forces, was also elected to the Committee. 'Bob' and Bill Lewis were to serve as long-time Committee members, Bill also sang in the Golden Jubilee concert, providing another valuable link to those early days of the choir. At this time the Secretary was P.G. Baker, a local businessman who on occasion did not mince his words!

In 1953 a young man, Dennis Attrill, was appointed as assistant secretary, with a view to his taking over the reins in 1954. Dennis gave exceptional service to the Choir, eventually retiring as Secretary in 1990 after 36 years.

During the early years the Secretary was the principal executive officer, and organised concerts as well as the day-to-day running of the Choir. Dennis continued to sing with the Choir as a second tenor until 2004, and attended concerts and joined in with the Afternoon Group when he was able. In 2001 Dennis achieved the impressive score of 50 years as a choir member. At his presentation he recalled that he was persuaded to join the choir by Bert Vickery, Chairman at that time. Dennis opted for First Tenor because 'it seemed the easier option notewise'.

Another example of long service to the choir is the late Ted Way who retired as Choir Librarian in 1996 after 35 years service, for many of those years also acting as the Stage Manager for Concerts.

Other long-serving Committee members have been Arthur Davey, who served as Treasurer from 1951 to 1979, resigning because of ill health. Jack Hingston was another member of St. Andrews Church Choir who served on the Committee in various posts. A founder member, he was first Librarian, then served as Vice-Chairman from 1949 -1951, and again from 1956 to 1958. He later became publicity officer for a year in 1973-1974. He also served on several Social Committees. He retired from the Choir in 1975. Ted Cullen, who joined the Choir in 1951, was elected to the Social Committee in 1967 and served in that post until 1979. He was also Chairman from 1969 to 1972, retiring from the Choir in January 1988.

Many committee members seem to have been "jack of all trades", turning their hands to all sorts of jobs. Thus another long-serving member, Geoff Ede, is recorded in the minutes as organising weekly Choir raffles in order to boost funds at a time when they had fallen dangerously low, and also organising Choir Dinners at the Albermarle Centre, which he cooked himself. Geoff also did a stint as Choir Secretary, particularly during the busy Golden Jubilee Year. Sadly, he died early in 2006 and so was unable to enjoy the succession of special events in the Diamond Jubilee Year.

Reg Griffiths made a big contribution to the choir, both as a committee member, and also by taking over the running of the Afternoon Group (a small section that entertained those who could not get out to concerts by performing in care homes and similar institutions) and developing its programme so that it was for many years an indispensable part of the Choir's activities. His influence continued after his sudden death by means of a generous legacy which was earmarked for a replacement electric piano.

Brian Reynolds was both Treasurer and Secretary, so far the only committee member to serve the Choir in both posts. He combined his duties with those of Stage Manager, succeeding Ted Way in the post, organising the actual arrangement of the members at Concerts, and ensuring that all singers can see the Conductor.

The post of Librarian is one that has become increasingly onerous as the repertoire and the number of members in the Choir has risen. In the early days, a membership of about two dozen, and a repertoire of about ten or at most a dozen pieces, meant that there were only about 250 pieces of music to be accounted for.

The slow rate of turnover also made the Librarian's job considerably easier. Alan Richards followed Ted Way in the post in 1996, and had to cope with the welcome problems associated with the large increase in choir numbers. Nowadays, members may be holding up to about forty pieces of music, about a third of which are changed every season, and if they were members of the Afternoon Group the extra music added to this volume of work considerably. Each season the Librarian may now find himself responsible for issuing and collecting up to 2500 pieces of music.

It is no wonder that it has been found necessary to appoint an assistant librarian for several years now, Dai Helps being the first holder of that office, and succeeding Alan, who stepped down to Assistant Librarian in 2005. Our recent Librarians Peter McKegney and Richard Venn continue the onerous task of not only managing the music scores but also engaging the choir and musical team in the often fractious task of culling some items and introducing new ones. Finalising the next year's programme on the ferry to France for our Lisieux trip allowed the librarian (your editor) to complete the task without a drawn out debate.

In the early days of the Choir, and for many years, almost until the retirement of Dennis Attrill, the Chairman was something of a sinecure, very much the convenor of the one or two committee meetings held each year. The Secretary was the executive officer, responsible for the normal running of the Choir, fixing concerts, engaging soloists, and purchasing music. Thus the redoubtable P.G. Baker scarcely regarded it as demotion when he was invited to become Secretary in 1951 in succession to Cyril Salway, having been Chairman for the previous two years.

Cyril remarked that it was one means of mitigating the abrasiveness of his tongue, which flailed conductors, members and audiences alike! Baker was also elected Deputy Musical Director. He retired from both his posts in 1954 when he left the area to live in Torquay.

Neither should the record of ordinary members of the Choir, who did not necessarily serve on the Committee, be forgotten. Many members have been members of the choir for twenty or thirty and more years. Tony Osmond, one of our cherished band of First Tenors, joined in 1974, and Gilbert Fairs, a Second Tenor, who joined in 1980, were both recruited from St. Andrew's Rowbarton. Charles Johnstone, second bass, joined in 1975, but did have some gaps in his membership when he was unable to sing with the Choir, but he remained a valued member of the second basses. Ted Rex, a first bass was a member from 1955 to 1983, and Cyril Vian, a second bass was another long-serving member from 1957 to 2003, and then occasionally singing with the Afternoon Group. Yet another St. Andrew's recruit was Ernie Glanville, who sang with the Choir for ten years from 1968 to 1978.

Recent members have joined the choir either through recruitment events or more often by invitation / cajoling from other members. Some arrive after researching the local area and finding that TDMVC is the only choir of its type for many miles around. Others have been introduced through their wives' association with local choirs.

President

The Choir has also been fortunate that its Presidents have all taken a keen interest in the welfare of the Choir, and often a considerable practical interest. This is particularly true of the present holder of that office, **David Gill**, who followed his father, the late Councillor **Willie Gill**. Since 1981 David has taken an active part in the affairs of the choir, attending committee meetings, and supporting the choir at its various concerts and events. Now retired, David was for many years a Principal of a local firm of Auctioneers and Estate Agents. He was also a local Councillor, as was his father before him, and served as Mayor of the new Borough of Taunton Deane in 1978 - 79.

The Choir has been lucky in having other notable Presidents. The first was **Victor Collins**, the newly elected Labour M.P. for Taunton in the 1945 General Election. He lost the seat in the 1952 Election, and moved away to contest the Shoreditch and Finchley seat in an Election in 1956, called because of the death of a sitting member. He lost this seat in 1959 to a young conservative candidate called Margaret Thatcher, and was elevated to the House of Lords, taking the title Lord Stonham.

J.A.D. Wilson succeeded Victor Collins as President in 1951, remaining in office until his death in 1964. He was a prominent local businessman, active in the Chamber of Commerce and Chairman for many years of Somerset Motors. He was a keen amateur musician, and often sang with the choir as a 'guest chorister'. In 1956 he was elected as Deputy Musical Director, although this post was abolished at the next A.G.M. in April 1957.

Sidney Holyoak, the County Music Advisor, had proved a good friend to the Choir ever since its early days, having been elected as a Vice President in 1959, and he proved a very active President from 1964 until his unexpected death in 1966. He had been responsible for encouraging the appointment of Ron Tickner as conductor in 1962 and one of his last services for the choir was to superintend the appointment of Douglas Shepherd. Holyoak was particularly interested in promoting choral singing, and Francis Burroughes, the musical director from 1992 to 2006, first met him when he was accompanist for a Festival of School Choirs which Holyoak organised in St. John's Church Yeovil in the late 1950s and early 1960s, little thinking thirty years later he would later come to conduct the Choir of which Holyoak was then President.

Our 75th Anniversary Year is also the 40th Anniversary of **David Gill** taking on the Chairmanship, a post the choir is delighted that he continues to hold and he supports us with such enthusiasm and wisdom.

David Gill, President 1981 to the present day

David has been an ever present and willing supporter of the choir. In 2006 he delivered a Diamond Jubilee Message that sums up his vital contribution.

"I am thrilled and honoured to write this message for our choir's Diamond Jubilee 60th Year Programme; I realise that it is a sign of getting older but to me it seems quite a short time ago that I wrote a message for the Golden Jubilee!

"Following my father's death in December 1980 I succeeded him as President in early 1981 – so I am celebrating my Silver Jubilee with the choir. During this long period I have tried my best to quietly assist and support successive Chairmen, Conductor, the Committee and our members in whatever ways I have been able.

"It is a source of much pride and continuing satisfaction that our choir has grown numerically. However it is also the improvement in quality of their singing and their performance that has surprised so many people. As a past Mayor, I know that the residents of Taunton Deane greatly appreciate our choir and are very proud of you, but nobody is prouder than I am.

"It is a tremendous achievement to have reached our 60th Anniversary (brought about by such loyalty and commitment) and to be still giving so much pleasure to our audiences and raising large sums of money for worthwhile charities. Keep up the good work!

"I commend with confidence our concerts for the 2005 – 2006 season, in which we are performing specifically to raise funds for four Somerset charities – SURE (*Somerset Unit for Radiotherapy Equipment*), Somerset Association for the Blind, Somerset Cancer Care and Children's Hospice South West, and trust that they will be enthusiastically supported. The choir will, of course, be assisting several other worthy causes in their fund-raising during the course of the 2005 – 2006 season.

"My sincere congratulations, best wishes and thanks to our officers, especially Chairman Tony Slavin, Committee, Choir members, Conductor and Accompanists."

Chairman of the Choir

The Chairmanship of the Choir seems to have been taken almost in rotation in those early years, few serving for any considerable length of time, until the reign of David Gledhill. He served from 1972 until 1988, and was succeeded by Wyn Davies, who remained in post until shortly before his death in 2003.

It was in David Gledhill's time that with the gradual increase in Choir membership and activities, the Chairman became much more active in giving impetus to the Choir. Committee meetings became more frequent, and the topics for discussion widened. In Wyn Davies's tenure Committee meetings increased to four a year, with various sub-committees, such as the Music sub-committee and the Golden Jubilee Committee, meeting as and when required.

Tony Slavin brought the administration of the Choir into the 21st. century by increasing the frequency of the meetings to five or six a year, and, in the lead up to the Diamond Jubilee celebrations, even more frequently, almost monthly. Tony had joined the Committee in 1997 as first bass representative and then in 1999 as Social Secretary. In 2001, he was elected Concert Secretary and editor of Voice-Male, the choir newsletter, roles he retained in addition to his Chairman's duties.

Tony Slavin, Chairman 2003 – 2015

Choir member since 1996 – in his own words.

"It never occurred to me when I was 'pressganged' into joining TDMVC in December 1995 at West Monkton Village Hall by John Blackmore, David Speight and Tony West that I would be rewarded by entering such a satisfying and enjoyable period of my life. Never having sung in a choir it was all new to me but as so many have discovered singing in a Male Voice Choir quickly becomes a way of life. In those days rehearsals were held in the hall of St Georges Junior School and continued there until 2004 when we moved to the Temple Methodist Church.

"Like all organisations the committee was always on the lookout for potential committee members and I was co-opted to the post of Social Secretary in 1997.

I succeeded Tony West as Editor of the Newsletter and in 2001 introduced a new Quarterly 12 page newsletter, Voice-Male. John Blackmore was a great help, initially doing the publishing. John Crosby enthusiastically took over the editorship in 2006. In 2001 I also filled the vacant post of Concert Secretary which I considered the most rewarding post on the committee. It gave me the opportunity to really learn what male voice choirs were all about, coming into contact with other choirs, their Chairmen and concert performers. I was always on the lookout for ideas and inspirations that could be applied beneficially to TDMVC. I still find it strange that no one at that time put themselves forward to fill this vacancy at the AGMs. Things were certainly moving very fast and the learning curve very steep but other committee members were very supportive and encouraging.

"It was with great sadness that Chairman, Wyn Davies, passed away in April 2003, having served in that position with distinction for 11 years. His wife, Meg, was granted Honorary Life Membership in recognition of Wyn's service to the Choir. I wrote in Voice-Male "Wyn was a man of immense character and presence (and even charm, when he wanted to be!). He brought dignity and credit to the Choir and was its finest ambassador". During his long illness the committee selected me as Acting Chairman, a position I occupied until being elected Chairman in June 2003. The committee approved my suggestion that Succession Planning should be adopted as standard practice in 2014 and I subsequently stepped down in June 2015 completing 12 years in that post and 14 years as Concert Secretary. Peter Verge should be thanked for putting such a valuable piece of procedure in place. What follows are some of my memories.

"Of course, Dr Francis Burroughes, choir MD, was an inimitable character with the highest musical standards, frustrated by "the lowest form of musical genre, male voice choir, other than Barbershop" to use his own 'humorous' words! Anyway, he couldn't be faulted for his perseverance and dedication over about 14 years. He undoubtedly raised the musicality and extended the range of music sung by the Choir. He commissioned two pieces of music for the choir to celebrate our Diamond Jubilee Year by Denys Hood and Alan Simmons, conductors of Male Voice Choirs who have branched out into arranging and composition. Denys Hood produced a tribute to Taunton Deane MVC in *The Perfect Male Voice Choir*. Alan Simmons produced an original work relating the story of

Irving Berlin. Simmons considers *Irving* one of his best pieces of writing, and was certainly an unusual and challenging addition to our repertoire.

"I wrote in Voice-Male following Francis's final appearance with the Choir in the Diamond Jubilee Concert "I'm sure we will not be able to match his 'quick change' at the end of the concert when the Choir were singing *Alexander's Ragtime Band*. After dashing stage left Francis re-appeared donned in 'slapper' gear and attempting to dance something like 'the Charleston'. To say it was memorable would not do the occasion justice. Not to be outdone, the Choir cut off Francis's exit and forced him to remain to listen to the most emotive rendition of *You'll Never Walk Alone* that he will ever hear. Not a few of us noticed a slight glistening in his eyes.

"The Choir Accompanist when I joined was Liz Bell who retired after 19 years in 2001. Robert Murray and then Jason Baxter held the position briefly before Hazel Reed joined us in 2003/4. We have been in awe of Hazel's playing ever since, she has been a stalwart and an essential part of all the choir's achievements. Thank you Hazel from everyone. It would be opportune to mention Valerie Hill too. She had been the Choir Accompanist, I believe, in the mid-Sixties whilst teaching at Weirfield and Taunton Junior School. After many years away, when she was recuperating from a stroke, Alan Richards approached her on behalf of the choir offering her the opportunity to become involved again. She was delighted and assisted in accompanying and teaching and eventually, as Assistant MD, conducted us on many occasions. Val too was considered a 'gem' by our members, being fastidious about following her conducting precisely! She specifically enjoyed teaching and conducting *The Rose* and *Let it be me*. Sadly she passed away in 2020 having suffered ill health for some time.

"In 2003 the choir numbered about 45 on paper but was effectively 41 and attendances were often in the 20's and 30's at rehearsals and concerts. I can recall occasions when only two top Tenors were on stage and sometimes just two or three Basses. Francis (Burroughes) had written an article in the Voice-Male just before he retired expressing the view that choirs don't have a God given right to exist and the advice that it's something that has to be continually worked at.

"Subsequently, the most significant decision taken during my early years as Chairman was to devise and implement a <u>Five Year Plan</u>. A questionnaire requesting information and views was undertaken, duly discussed by a sub-committee and reported to the committee before being presented to the choir in August 2003. TDMVC was fortunate in having in its midst a core of very committed members who wholeheartedly endorsed the report and this enabled the Five Year Plan to be launched and form the basis for good practice for running the choir business, future planning and the development of the choir.

"The essence of the Plan was to 1) ensure the survival of the choir 2) raise choral skills and presentation standards and seek more prestigious concert venues 3) share concerts with other male voice and female choirs, and <u>aim to sing without music copy</u> thereby matching other significant choirs 4) undertake tours and festivals with adequate preparation and planning 5) select music that was progressive and entertaining. Each of these headings were split into subsections too numerous to detail here.

"Once the Plan was implemented progress was made on all fronts and there was feedback to the choir on a regular basis both verbally and in Voice-Male and a progress report presented at each AGM. The final achievement was for the choir to sing without copy and that happened officially in February 2009 in Creech St Michael Village Hall. Initially the front row undertook to sing without copy whilst the second and third rows progressed more slowly. A great deal of discussion had taken place with arguments presented either way, but with guidance and encouragement a strong desire emerged to succeed. MD David Yates was instrumental in getting us there, no mean task.

"It would be poignant to express here our gratitude to David Yates, our former MD, who succeeded Francis Burroughes, for his efforts and perseverance in getting us to this point. Following Francis's retirement, for which he'd given us 3 years notice, attempts to recruit an MD had proved unsuccessful and we found ourselves without an MD. David, who at the time was a chorister (T2) bravely presented himself to take on the role, on a trial basis, having only a limited amount of experience. His offer was accepted and his position verified in January 2007. All choir members are eternally grateful to David, he enabled us to continue following our dreams.

"During the summer of 2005 I enrolled on a basic website design course, then with the assistance of someone I knew the first Choir Website was launched in

October 2005. It was well received and over time improved. Initially I managed the site and, again, was assisted by Adam Green, a friend of John Crosby. Finally, I enlisted the help of Martin Howe of IT Know Howe as the site became more sophisticated. We were really in the technical age now! Since those days we have seen a major advance in the design of the site.

"A variety of initiatives were embarked on to meet the aims of our Plan. In order to help develop confidence in our ability to perform publicly, at our social events individuals were encouraged to sing, recite or play. We discovered a wide range of soloists and duets in our midst. The events proved very popular and attendances were high. Perhaps it was the tasty American Suppers that were the attraction. Popular venues were The White Horse, Bradford-on Tone; The Royal Oak, Hillcommon; Staplegrove Village Hall and the new Oake Village Hall. This approach was complimented by an annual Garden Party held in member's gardens. John Pinkard, Alf Anstee and John Crosby generously offered to host us and I can recall that we always had good weather!

"Another initiative was to organise Workshops led by expert choral and voice teachers. The first, in 2004, led by a renowned MD, Sheila Harrod, of the Kentwood Show Choir, Swindon headlined our summer recruitment drive at Queen's College in 2004. This was followed by an Open Evening later on and the end result was 12 new members. The extra effort and expense proved to be worthwhile. We continued inviting high calibre workshop leaders like Roy Wales (Cornwall International MVC Festival Director), Penny Jenkins (Ardingly College), Angela Renshaw (Holman Climax MVC, Cornwall), Paul Triggs (City of Truro MVC) and Mark Burstow (Bournemouth MVC). Our final workshop was in 2015, a collaboration between our MD, Nick Thomas, and local operatic star, Alison Kettlewell. Alison, primarily a voice coach/ teacher, remarked "the boys were attentive, polite, engaged and made me feel really welcome....... I certainly found it a rewarding experience ..." There's got to be a message there!

"Additionally, several Open Evenings were organised, in varying formats, when male members of the public were invited to join us on our rehearsal evening to experience the joy of singing in a MVC. This was generally making use of our own musicians but I recall two occasions when invited tutors ran the proceedings. Several of our members also sang with The Rivertones, a Taunton based barbershop group, and I was extended an invitation by Chairman Colin

Harlow to attend their practices to experience coaching and singing techniques delivered by experts in their genre of choral music. I was immediately impressed by the quality of teaching and techniques and arranged for them to lead three Open Evening Workshops in 2008 for TDMVC which resulted in several new members. Another, in early 2012 led by Penny Jenkins at the Taunton Baptist Church resulted in another influx of twelve choristers.

"We looked to broaden our horizons by performing joint concerts with other male voice choirs and in more prestigious venues. It was important to team up with choirs that we knew might be better than us so that we would be encouraged to emulate them and not to feel intimidated. Over time we did genuinely feel this transformation and that made us even more determined to succeed.

"I thought it was important to forge relationships with choirs in our region and that led to performing with Budleigh Salterton and Barnstaple MVCs on several occasions, two choirs that set a good example of the standard we should match early in our development and I'm delighted to say that we did just that. In those early years we also performed joint concerts with Basingstoke, Bournemouth, Swindon, Marazion Apollo, St Austell and City of Truro. Several of these attended the Cornwall International Festival and gave us the opportunity to socialise as friends. I have to say that within my choir roles I looked forward to sharing platforms with these choirs because of the assurance it gave me that we were on track to achieve our ambitions.

"In 2003 the choir first attended the Concert of Brass & Voices at the Royal Albert Hall in aid of Cancer Research. It was Jack Dennis's drive and enthusiasm that got this triennial pilgrimage underway, later to be taken on by John Capell. If my calculations are correct our sixth appearance was in 2018. There is no doubt that this has been the most prestigious venue where the choir has performed. Each RAH trip holds individual memories for choristers I'm sure.

"During the Millennium Year the Choir travelled to Manchester and sang at a massed choir event in the massive Manchester Evening Standard Arena and organised its own massed choir event at Wells Cathedral attended by 400 choristers.

"Our Choir has had a significant presence at the Cornwall International MVC Festival starting in 2007 and making 5 appearances up to 2019. I recall in 2007 that at the very last minute our designated hotel decided that it was not able to accommodate us so I had to scrabble around searching alternative hotels all over Cornwall. I couldn't believe my luck when I discovered the Travelodge in St Austell, where we were to perform, had the 38 bedrooms we required for our party of over 70. This number was exceeded in 2009 when a party of 91 travelled to Cornwall. What relief! In my mind our most memorable performance of all our Cornwall visits occurred in 2013 when I received an urgent call from the Festival Director, Peter Davies, asking if we would be prepared to sing in Truro Cathedral as a late replacement for a German choir. It meant leaving earlier in the day so that we could perform en route at 1.00pm. The choir responded positively and we set off in uniform ready to take the stage.

"Fortunately, we were the third and final choir on stage so we had a little time to compose ourselves. I still recall Carol conducting the choir in a warm-up in the town car park before heading off to the Cathedral. We performed *Anthem* and *Divine Brahma* particularly well and received the best ovation of the concert. No mean feat when the two other overseas choirs were amongst the elite at the Festival. If you're interested you can view part of the performance on YouTube. John Larke, City of Truro Chairman and the concert Presenter, sent a favourable report on our performance to the Festival Director.

"We have, of course, extensive memories of the singing, socialising and camaraderie because of these ventures. This has contributed enormously to us being the choir we are today - a choir primarily based on friendship that incorporated our wives and partners. Our Ladies support us in so many ways, firstly by being honest critics of our performances, always well represented at our concerts wherever they were and whatever time of the year and providing and serving the astonishing teas we offered which were so appreciated by our guest choirs. Our Ladies' contributions were never bettered wherever we travelled I can assure you. Pamela Lucas was the first leader of the group, later to be followed by Carol Anstee.

"Annual Concerts tend to be the showpiece for all male voice choirs and ours grew in stature in each successive year. St Andrew's Church from 1947 to 1995, and then The Brewhouse until 2000 prior to moving to The Tacchi- Morris Arts Centre in June 2001. This was a decision taken by the committee based on economic reasons – it was just too expensive to book The Brewhouse. We quickly settled in our new home and we created a remarkable connection with the place because of the memories of performances, audiences, soloists and musicians and the search for variety of content.

"Concert titles were introduced trying to capture the musical theme of the evening with visual images projected on the stage background, resulting in 'Stouthearted Men', 'The Roving Kind', 'Men Aloud', 'Some Enchanted Evening' and 'Let All Men Sing', etc. There were a succession of wonderful and popular soloists, Mary Morgan, Hilary Glenny, Rhiannon Llewellyn, Frances Walker, Louise Innes and Alison Kettlewell to name a few. Choir members also contributed in different ways with Terry Stirzaker, as Fagin, *Reviewing the Situation* and John Capell a stirring *Galloping Major*. It was also a delight to have Tenor, Jonathan Farey and his Farey Family perform their own compositions which never failed to captivate audiences.

"Our ambitions grew to the extent that for several years from 2006 to 2012 musical sketches were performed by Choir members, wives and partners and guests. Namely *Master of the House* from Les Miserables, and songs from *Oklahoma* and *Fiddler on the Roof*. Kevin Baker was instrumental in putting these together and it was a fun time, but we moved on.

We took advantage of the recording facilities at the Tacchi-Morris, the Technician supplied us with the recorded disc at the end of the evening and John Blackmore excellently produced cased CDs with illustrated sleeves which resulted in useful income for choir funds each year. It was customary to list the names of all choir members in the Annual Concert programme and it is noteworthy that in June 2015 there were 15 x T1s, 25 x T2s, 23 x B1s & 17 x B2s, totalling a record 80 choristers!

"A notable event during this period of choir history was the Inaugural Patronage Concert for the Mayor of Taunton Deane, Cllr Bob Bowrah, BEM, on the 20th March 2010 in The Temple Methodist Church. It was enriched by the presence of Barnstaple MVC, the joint choir combining to produce a magnificent sound and spectacle. The idea of approaching the Mayor to become our Patron was the consequence of a visit by Swindon MVC whose Patron was their Mayor. It seemed such a good idea and has resulted in mutual benefit to both parties. It has added to our prestige and local recognition and the Mayor's charities have benefited from the proceeds of the Patron's annual concerts.

"Significant sums of money have been raised for several military charities, specifically, 'Go Commando' (Help for Heroes), 2012, SSAFA Armed Forces Day, 2013 & 2015, 6 Rifles, Care for Casualties, 2013 and The Army Benevolent Fund, 2014. And, of course, WW1 & WW11 commemorative concerts in the following years.

"Early records in 2002 show that the choir raised £3500 for charity but by 2009 this had risen to £5500. Then from 2012 – 2015 a total of £42000 was contributed to worthy causes. The overall total for this period must have exceeded £80000. A record we can be truly proud of.

"Concerts, of course, don't just happen. Many people contribute to a successful outcome. Namely Brian Reynolds and Alf Anstee who have been our only Stage Managers to date. Alf along with Jeff Garland have been the 'tour de force' of storing, organising and erecting our staging. The staging was purchased in 2013/14 at a cost of £4794 plus more than £2000 for a trailer. We were fortunate in obtaining a community grant of about a third from Taunton Deane Borough Council.

"Our Concert Presenters, introduced in 2012, were Steve Jones and Alan Hooper and they have been followed by John Bentley, Barry Havenhand and Phil Knowles. It goes without saying that their presence has added an air of distinction and good humour to our concert performances.

"The Choir had an active afternoon choir, The 'Reg Griffiths Singers', when I joined in 1996 and in which up to 20 choir members sang regularly. Welshman Reg Griffiths was a life-sized character He had conducted the choir for a year or so prior to Francis Burroughes' arrival. When Reg passed away in around 1999 the ensemble was manged by Alan Richards and then Brian Reynolds. The conductor was Audrey Silke and the pianists were Joan Saunders and Dora Brooks. This group performed around 20 to 25 afternoon concerts annually, singing its own repertoire. I regard its appearance in the 2006 Jubilee Concert singing a medley from 'South Pacific' as being the pinnacle of its achievements. The Afternoon Entertainers, as they became known, performed all over Taunton Deane in village, church and community halls for different kinds of groups and societies and contributed over £300 annually to the Choir finds from the donations received. Members of the group sang solos and duets, recited monologues and poetry. Regretfully, in 2011 it was decided to disband the Entertainers as there wasn't a volunteer to take over its organisation.

"Towards the end of 2007 I was approached by the Rev Rod Corke of St Mary's, Taunton enquiring if the Choir would like to sing at a wedding which the church choir was unable to fulfil. The choir was enthusiastic when I put it to them and that was the first of several over the following seven years. Each occasion was enjoyable and sociable and the Choir was extended invitations to have tea or take refreshments etc after the ceremony. We travelled to Enmore, Luccombe, Pitney, St Audries West Quantoxhead and a few around Taunton and Wellington. The ceremony and setting at St Audries was quite special and the weather was good! I was able to negotiate a fee and recover travel expenses for choir members in each instance; useful income for the Choir.

"A topic which seems have been discussed ad infinitum and still unresolved is the choir uniform and I , for my sins, was not able to resolve it either. I once felt we, the committee, were on track to achieving a good outcome having introduced a new blazer badge, tie, jubilee shirt and provided a standardised pair of grey worsted trousers for all choir members. With just the blazer remaining and a survey of the choir showing well over 90% support for the proposal it appeared a foregone conclusion. At the 2011 AGM a new dark blue blazer was displayed and a financial package for the members to vote on. Following much discussion and due amendment to the committee proposal it was surprisingly defeated and I fail to understand why to this day. I sympathise with the Herculean task before the current committee and all future committees in resolving this eternal problem.

"As mentioned above Choir performances had been recorded on quite a few occasions and expertly transferred to CD by John Blackmore and supplied to members for a small charge which went into choir funds. So, in 2010 we took up the challenge of having a recording made professionally by Steve Swinden who was in the area doing the same for Minehead MVC. The recording took place in St Michael's Church, Galmington over two Saturday sessions with 51 choristers contributing. It was launched at our Annual Concert 2010 and titled 'Sung from the Heart'. Local artist, Constance Milburn, consented to her paintings of Taunton scenes being used to illustrate the CD cover. Initial sales enabled the outlay to be recovered over a couple of years and the balance over a further couple. We ventured into a second recording in 2015 with 'Let All Men Sing' recorded in St James Church, Taunton. 66 choristers contributed in this instance. The cover consisted of a collage of photographs taken by John Blackmore. Sales were initially good but it took some time to recover our outlay and I believe it discouraged us from making a further recording.

"I think the experience was worthwhile and enjoyed by most singers although I found the making of the second recording quite demanding. We have to thank John Capell, Bill Hubbock and John Hassall for taking charge of the CD sales to our members and at concerts, ably assisted by others.

"Just for sentimental reasons I wish to recall the several Christmas concerts we performed at the Albemarle Centre, Taunton. We looked forward to the sheer delight on the faces of our audiences as we sang, in our Santa hats, from our repertoire, carols with audience participation and guest performers and choir members adding to the Christmas flavour. Regrettably, when Manager Shirley Hector retired the show came to an end. Happy memories...

"We shouldn't forget the many devoted followers that the Choir accumulated over this period some of whom I have seen at our more recent concerts, but time is taking its toll. Some became Friends of the Choir and paid a small subscription which contributed over £300 annually and assured a good audience at our annual concerts. Carol Anstee acted as secretary for the Friends and also assisted me in producing Choir statistics from the weekly register taken by Alf Anstee which were presented annually at our AGM.

"Our former Musical Director, David Yates, with typical selflessness, accelerated his retirement in 2013 to accommodate the appointment of his successor, Nick Thomas, who had become 'available'. I had been tracking Nick for a few years but, as we all know, he's a very busy man with many commitments and was also in great demand on the Taunton music scene. Having had trial conducting opportunities at St Mary's Church, Taunton and the Barnstaple MVC annual concert in May and July 2013 he was happy to accept our invitation to become our more than worthy Musical Director. That was 7 years ago, my how time flies. Nick has been so good for our choir, improving voice projection and tone, presentation and performance. He is a highly accomplished flautist and makes a unique contribution to our concerts which is much admired by our audiences. Nick has inspired us to new heights; onwards and upwards.

"And the person who, I believe, has the longest connection with TDMVC is our very special President, David Gill. David succeeded his father in 1981 as President and the Choir has benefited because of the care and attention David has given to his roll. He attends many of our local concerts in addition to the larger, more prestigious fundraising events for major charities and hosts the dignitaries and guests. When I was Chairman he was my greatest supporter and advocate and he was so generous to the choir without wishing to draw attention to himself. David has been President of The Rowbarton Friendship Association for a great number of years and a section of the Choir has regularly led the carol singing at their Christmas Lunch. TDMVC has been most fortunate to have this very special person as its President.

"I have already named people by describing the ways in which they have served the Choir during my tenure. But there are others also worthy of mention who contributed to the achievements and advancements over this most progressive period. Alf Anstee who served as my Vice-Chairman, Jeff Garland (Choir Rep and Uniform Officer), Brian Lucas (Treasurer), Alan Richards & Dai Helps (Librarians), Roger Sleap (Choir Rep and Welfare), John Pinkard (Social Secretary), Ray Butler (Concert Ticket sales), Steve Reid (Publicity & PR) & Stuart Gifford (Secretary).

"I would like to conclude, if you will grant me the liberty, of saying 'thank you' to my wife Carol for her total support during my years of service to TDMVC. It has always been a labour of love and will provide us both with some of the happiest memories of our lives."

Carol Slavin quote: "I always think of the Choir as Tony's mistress but fortunately I like her!" (May 2015)

John Capell, Chairman from 2015 - 2018

"My choir story began in Bishops Lydeard post office where Ruth, my wife, was briefly shopping on the way home from work. She spotted a postcard advertisement trying to recruit choristers to Taunton Deane Male Voice Choir. She came home to tell me about this and as they say the rest is history!

I joined the choir in the late nineties and immediately appreciated the warmth and camaraderie that has always surrounded our organisation. My first memories are of the Musical Director, Francis Burroughes and the chairman Wynn Davies. Very quickly I realised that there was a considerable Welsh influence and I learnt to be confident singing my part between Dai Helps and John Thomas, two excellent Welsh voices and undoubtedly my early mentors. I can vividly remember, at my first rehearsal, wondering at the interval what kind of organisation I was considering joining as Wynn gave a medical report on ailing members of the choir! His booming bass voice was unmistakeable. I remember wondering whether there were enough fit members to sing!

I also remember Dr Burroughes as an outstanding musician who insisted on accuracy. However, this sometimes led to note bashing rehearsals that were hard to endure. My first concert was in Ilminster at the Quaker Hall. I was amazed at the size of the audience – including a few wives there were only 8 (eight) which was probably half the number in the choir! I also remember that it was always difficult to recruit top tenors – sometimes we only had one, although he had a great solo voice!

"Francis Burroughes was followed by David Yates as our MD, stepping up from the second tenors, when we were unable to recruit externally. David led us towards singing 'without copy', though many were reticent and reluctant to take the plunge. The choir made strides forward under his leadership and he certainly ensured the longevity of the choir at a time when we needed a Musical Director to continue as a choir. David was succeeded by Nick Thomas, who has undoubtedly improved the choir enormously. Many concerts where Nick has conducted have been some of the best that our choir has performed in all the years that I have been a member.

"Our choir has changed beyond all recognition over the last 20 years. It has grown in size but especially in quality. In fact, with Nick as our MD, I now leave rehearsals with a spring in my step and yet another good tune in my head.

"I first joined the committee as a section representative, moving on to Librarian in 2011 and then to Chairman in 2015. From 2013 to 2015, a great deal of work was undertaken to develop a succession plan that would move the choir forward into an exciting new era. There were a number of members who worked tirelessly, behind the scenes, in a multitude of meetings, resulting in reports and final proposals. Peter Verge, John Blackmore, John Capell, Steve Reed and Tony Moore were probably the main workers. Our succession plan now ensures that all committee positions are time limited, which results in new blood, fresh ideas and differing approaches to each post. Our choir has undoubtedly grown stronger in terms of management and quality in the past six years."

Paull Robathan, Chairman 2018 - 2021

It is always a bit difficult to write dispassionately about oneself, so I will be brief and factual.

Some time before 2014 I attended a concert by Stanchester Quire held in the church in my village of South Petherton. After the concert one of the choir members approached me and said that I was obviously singing along so much I should really join the choir....something that had not occurred to me in recent years, even though I sang in two part and four part choirs at school in South Wales.

I thought little of the suggestion until I attended another concert at the same church, but this time it was Taunton Deane Male Voice Choir. I was hooked. Shortly afterwards I contacted the Chairman Tony Slavin and was invited to a rehearsal. I joined immediately, and have never regretted it. (The choir might have done).

When John Capell became Chairman in 2015 the position of Librarian became vacant and considering it less complex and time consuming than Treasurer or Secretary I offered myself, and was duly appointed. With help from the previous Librarian and others we attacked the mass of sheet music extracting any rogue photocopies and auditing numbers of copies.

The new Musical Director, Nick Thomas, looked for some new music and we purchased several songs that we sing today. The selection of which songs to go into the repertoire fell to the Music Committee made up from a representative from each section, the Musical Director, Librarian and Vice Chairman. Our most successful selection year culminated in a meeting on board the ferry to France for our trip to Lisieux - a captive audience is a useful thing at times.

Tony Slavin had created an excellent website for the choir but times move on and it was ready for an update. With some experience in this area I developed a WordPress based new website that I am delighted that Chris Evans took on after a time and is making a much better job of it than I ever would.

In 2018 I was elected Chairman and looked forward to three years of 'normality' with a stable musical team, growing choir and great energy in the group. My first report to the choir in June 2018 already was looking forward to 2021 and the 75th Anniversary, along with visits already planned to the Royal Albert Hall, Holland and Wells Cathedral where we combined with Glastonbury, Mendip and the Somerset and Avon Police Choir and 150+ voices raised the roof and a sizeable sum of money.

I committed to dedicate a very large percentage of my life for the next three years. A few things got in the way of that, a heart attack, open heart surgery and Covid-19 but we saw our way through all of them and have come out the other side strong and united.

I wish my successor Jeff Garland all the very best, he has a new chapter to write in the choir's development and I have no doubt he will make a fine job of it.

One key activity during my tenure was the advancement of the 2020 Vision. A working party set up during 2016 did exceptional work in identifying, characterising and commenting on all key aspects of the choir. A review of the Vision in 2017 confirmed the main areas where emphasis could be placed to advance our common goal of 'being recognised as the best male voice choir in the South West by 2020'

Covering everything from singing quality, including discipline in rehearsals and on stage, voice assessments, sectional practice, public presentation, uniform, recruitment and fellowship the working party was made up of Alan Hooper, John Blackmore, Steve Jones, Phil Knowles and Derek Parsons.

The work to deliver all the recommendations is not over. The uniform remains a continuing debate with no clear favoured way forward. For other aspects we have improved but there is always scope for more.

Covid-19 has taken us out of our comfort zone, and is not done yet, but when we are back on an even keel I have no doubt that the choir can work together towards the common goal of continuous improvement in all areas.

11 THE AFTERGLOW AND FARMER'S BOY

What is an afterglow? The Oxford Dictionary defines it as "the light that is left in the sky after the sun has set" or "a pleasant feeling after a good experience".

A successful concert leaves singers with a good "glowing" feeling, particularly when singing jointly with other choirs, and this is often extended after the concert has finished - an experience known as the 'Afterglow', when the opportunity is taken to socialise with visiting choir members and their supporters.

After a drink and a chat comes the inevitable singing - always a different selection to the one just sung in the concert . At Taunton Deane we often start with our signature song - *The Farmer's Boy,* a popular English country song a version of which was included by Robert Bell in his 'Ancient Poems Ballads and Songs of the Peasantry of England' published in 1857. *The Farmer's Boy* is sometimes included in our concert repertoire and will have an airing at the Rowbarton Concert in December 2021, reflecting Somerset's prominence as a farming community. It is interesting to note that the song immediately after *The Farmers' Boy* in Bell's book is a version of *Richard of Taunton Deane*!

Our selection of Afterglow songs includes sea shanties and folk songs, and such items as *Sloop John B*, and *Swing Low Sweet Chariot, Bread of Heaven*, and many others. It is always good to hear offerings from guest and host choirs, and we sometimes join in with each other's selections. Other choirs have different 'staples', Cowbridge Male Voice Choir regaled us with Max Boyce's *Hymns and Arias* which is of course well known by Welsh rugby fans and others across the world. The Afterglow is augmented by the talents of the Blackdown Hillbillies; Mike Fortune, Stuart Gifford, Alan Hooper and Phil Knowles who carry on the tradition of breakout groups from the main choir and delight audiences across the Blackdown Hills and beyond.

Afterglow venues are varied - for our annual concert at the Tacchi Morris Centre the afterglow takes place in the theatre bar, but for concerts elsewhere in the Taunton area we visit public houses such as the Vivary Arms in Taunton, the Worlds End in Bradford-on-Tone, and the Stragglers Bar at Somerset County Cricket Club.

When singing further afield arrangements are made by our host choir, and we have found ourselves singing in places such as Wells Rugby Club, a college in Rotterdam, and enjoying pasties at the St Austell Brewery. These occasions also give us the opportunity to listen to a wide range of other choirs, some from overseas, and some exceptional such as the Swiss Boys' Choir.

Sometimes these affairs are more formal; for example, when visiting France to sing in Taunton's twin town of Lisieux we enjoyed a post-concert meal in a hotel with our host families, and joined with them in a lot of singing.

We meet every Wednesday to rehearse. What better than to repair to the local pub The Vivary Arms where after 2 hours of intense singing practice we often ... sing, with a relaxing glass of something. The Vivary has hosted Afterglow with Ilminster Belles that matched the equivalent in Ilminster's Warehouse Theatre Bar with the same ladies.

These occasions are always very enjoyable, wherever they are held. So, when you attend a male voice choir concert, keep your ear to the ground, find out where the Afterglow is to be held, and get yourself down there - you could be in for a pleasant surprise!

12 THE ROSE

In one way at least the start of our 76th year is similar to the start of the choir itself. Covid-19 has made a massive impact on all of us. Many lives (too many) have been lost and few families have been unaffected in some way or other.

Reforming the choir and singing together for the first time in September was a milestone that felt like the beginning of a new era. Jeff Garland has taken on the role of Chairman and brings a wealth of experience and not a little humour to the task. We all wish him well.

In October we looked forward to our first concert while joining old and new friends at our 75th Anniversary Dinner at Oake Manor Golf Club. It was wonderful to see Ron Troup in his choir uniform from 'the old days' and Dr Francis Burroughes. Many former choir members joined us to listen to The Farey Family (maybe Jonathan will come back to the choir one day).

The title song from Bette Midler's film *The Rose* epitomises rebirth, and is a favourite song not only of the choir but also our audiences. Many a tear has been shed at concerts...

"Just remember in the winter, far beneath the bitter snows
Lies the seed that, with the sun's love, in the spring becomes
The Rose"

Our first three concerts after lockdown and other restrictions will all be in Taunton. First we will sing at the Tacchi Morris in our annual concert, then join with Taunton Rotary for a musical tribute to those who served.

We will end 2021 with our 75th Anniversary Concert at St Andrews Church, Rowbarton. Rowbarton is where this journey began and the concert will symbolise and re-affirm the connection the choir has with the local communities of Taunton Deane.

There are many more concerts to come and many new friends to make, both from our audience and from other choirs, who are about now also making a return from the privations of the virus.

All of this is for the next major anniversary. 100 years of Taunton Deane Male Voice choir. Many of us, including your author, will be very surprised if they are still around to witness and celebrate but from where we stand now the choir is set to grow in stature and numbers giving joy to audiences.

Delivering the message we use as our mission for our choir members and for all who think about singing with us.....

Singing can improve your health and happiness

Come and join us.

75th Anniversary Choir Members

First Tenors

Keith Gibbons
Mike Groves
Mac Muir
Derek Parsons
Huw Phillips
Gareth Rowlands
Graham Salter
Richard Salter
Iain Scotter
Terry Stirzaker
Chris Taylor
David Taylor
Ron Williams

Second Tenors

John Capell
David Corry
Bob Cowling
Chris Evans
Mike Fortune
Barry Havenhand
Dai Helps

John Hudson
Ivor Hussey
Derek Lawrence
Francis Lewis
Peter McKegney
Andrew Molan
Jim Nicol
Brian Parkes
Larry Pickard
Malcolm Phillips
Tony Slavin
Simon Stretton
Gareth Thomas
Richard Venn
Richard Walker
Tim Webster
Gerry Wells-Cole
Dennis Williams
Evan Williams

First Basses (Baritones)

Terry Abbiss
Alf Anstee
Keith Briars
Ray Butler
Jack Dennis
Stuart Gifford
Charles Hill
Alan Hooper
David Kelly
Philip Knowles
Martin Langford
Tony Moore
Rob Morgan
Paul Oates

Martyn Powe
Lukasz Pozarski
James Spradbery
Peter Wheeler
Gordon Willetts

Second Basses

David Capell
Trevor Davies
Jeff Garland
John Hassall
Duncan Hughes
Steve Jones
Jim Leach
Richard Kilbey
Paddy O'Boyle
John Pengelly
Martin Read
Steve Read
Paull Robathan
Tony Smith

Life Members

Life Membership is awarded in recognition of outstanding service that choir members have given to the Choir. They receive copies of the Choir's Newsletter, Voice-Male and regular invitations to the Choir's concerts and social functions.

Those who have been so honoured by the Choir are

Chris White, Musical Director
Dr Francis Burroughes, Musical Director
David Yates, Musical Director

Liz Bell and Valerie Hill for their service as Accompanists,

Dennis Attrill, the late Geoff Ede, David Gledhill and Cyril Vian for their contribution as officers and committee members. Brian Reynolds, Tony Osmond, David Gledhill, Alan Richards, Tony Slavin and John Blackmore

Meg Davies was also given a Life Membership in recognition of her late husband's Chairmanship.

ABOUT THE AUTHOR

Paull Robathan

Paull Robathan was Chairman of Taunton Deane Male Voice Choir from 2018 to 2021. He is grateful to the choir for not only for welcoming him as a shaky Baritone, but also for supporting his move to the Bass section where he hopefully does less damage.

Paull's involvement as Editor in the creation of this book has been based on the strong foundation built by Jack Dennis; by Voice-Male editors Dr John Crosby, John Blackmore and Ron Williams. There is no room to list everyone who has contributed – specific contributions are recognised in the main body of the book where possible, but so many deserve a huge vote of thanks for digging in to their memory banks and cupboards to haul out nuggets of facts that all combine (hopefully) to give this history a lively and rich flavour.

All errors and omissions are mine, and while I hope there are few errors there is a mass of material that has been omitted. It will all be available from the choir's archive.

Printed in Great Britain
by Amazon

71900808R00085